DEVELOPMENTS IN INTERPERSONAL SKILLS TRAINING

Developments in Interpersonal Skills Training

DON BINSTED
University of Lancaster

Gower

Published by
Gower Publishing Company Limited,
Gower House, Croft Road, Aldershot, Hampshire,
England.

and
Gower Publishing Company Limited,
Old Post Road, Brookfield, Vermont, 05036
USA.

ISBN 0 566 00827 0

Printed in Great Britain by Paradigm Print,
Gateshead, Tyne & Wear

Contents

1 Introductions

<u>What this monograph is about, the basis from</u>
<u>which it has been developed, the elements it</u>
<u>contains, and some of the dilemmas it will</u>
<u>confront. Its relevance to professional</u>
<u>development.</u>

INTRODUCTION

This monograph is written for trainers, teachers
involved in adult education, and managers and
supervisors who wish to develop their subordinates.
This statement to some extent defines the scope of
the contents, and the background from which it has
been developed. You will find that a number of
assumptions are implied in what follows.

The first is that the people whose interpersonal
skills are to be developed are in work, or are
preparing for work. This assumption has two
important implications:

    (a)   that the skills are set in some context
           and will have some specific foci and
           objectives. In general this will be an

organisational context which may be
complex and exhibit a distinctive culture
or way of going about things (e.g.
training people in company 'A' to deal
with complaints about their products);

(b)   that there is a motive for improving
people's interpersonal skills, for
example, to increase confidence or
effectiveness.

The second assumption is that the development of
skills will be facilitated by some person who may
be called trainer, teacher, manager or supervisor.
Although most of the monograph is written making
this assumption, the important issue of skill
development in 'self-development' groups will be
covered in Chapter 18.

There is no reason why many of the ideas and
practices described in this monograph could not be
used in other situations, such as training young
people for work, or for learning social skills in
schools. Clearly different assumptions would need
to be made about the learners. However, I have had
no experience of using the approaches to be
described in later chapters in these areas, nor
have I done research in areas other than 'in work'.

WHAT THE MONOGRAPH SETS OUT TO DO

The purpose of this monograph is to act as a guide
to trainers, teachers, managers and supervisors to
enable them to facilitate better the development of
interpersonal skills in others. At this point it
will be useful to use the collective noun
'facilitators' (facilitators of interpersonal skill
development) instead of trainers, teachers, etc..
There are three elements within the text.

Element 1 is the presentation of relevant theory.
The theories which are appropriate are to do with
learning and the design of effective learning
processes. They are relevant because they shed
light on the central process of learning, and thus
provide a basis for both designing effective skill
development activities and monitoring what is going

on in a learner group. The way in which theory can be applied to practical learning situations will be demonstrated by example.

Element 2 will be the presentation of new and modified practice. In essence this will be concerned with how to design, set up and run skill development sessions. This will involve describing some new approaches and designs and comparing these with what might be called the more traditional approaches to interpersonal skill development. It will become clear that ideas and practice from the 'new' approaches can be integrated into more 'traditional' designs.

Element 3 will be some self-development activities which are intended to help you to explore your present practice and your comfort with some different approaches. It must be emphasised that this is not a distance learning package, but more will be said about that in Chapter 18.

These three elements stem from various researches which my colleagues and I have carried out in the Centre for the Study of Management Learning at the University of Lancaster, over a number of years. These have been focussed in the management area of training and education. The practice described has been used and tested out in a number of different situations, sometimes with trainers, sometimes with managers or mixtures of the two. There are also comments on problems people have found when applying these ideas in an organisation (Chapter 17).

SOME GENERAL OBSERVATIONS

Developing interpersonal skills in others is an area in which many of us have worked over the years with greater or lesser success. In the past I have personally experienced considerable anguish over my own ineffectiveness in influencing people's interpersonal skills. Observation of colleagues and research into the design and implementation of a number of learning activities convince me that the whole field is neither well understood nor is the practice at a high standard.

Some of the dilemmas which present themselves to facilitators include:

- whether to use small group training sessions or one-to-one coaching;

- when it is appropriate to use highly structured activities, and when to use unstructured activities;

- the use of facilitator manufactured tasks, role plays, exercises, etc. compared with using learner's own experience;

- the degree to which the facilitator can enhance learning by careful debriefing, giving of feedback, etc. compared with allowing the group to unpack its own experience;

- the influence the facilitator will have on 'teaching people the right way to behave' compared with the group making up its own mind and in particular individuals making up their own minds about what behaviour is most important to them;

- how to use video feedback in such a way that it does not solely confirm the learners' inadequacies, but rather gives them ideas about what to do differently;

- whether to attempt to change attitudes to change behaviour or change behaviour as the preliminary to changing attitudes;

- to what extent people learn best by doing it 'wrong' so that they can be to told how to do it 'right'.

I will endeavour to confront these and suggest ways of helping facilitators to make informed choices.

THE RELEVANCE TO MANAGEMENT SUPERVISION AND PROFESSIONAL DEVELOPMENT

The approaches to be described are applicable to a wide variety of interpersonal skills. For example a retail shop assistant dealing with a

customer complaint, a representative introducing a
new drug to a medical practitioner or a manager
putting an awkward proposition to a union
shop-steward. Two types of application have
particular potential:

(a)   helping managers, supervisors or other
        professionals to improve their own
        interpersonal skills. Management people
        are mostly required to be people of
        action. Clearly this is not only a
        management prerogative, nor does it imply
        that 'thinking' is not a vital component
        of 'acting'. It is not a question of
        'action being a substitute for thought'
        but of 'action being required to achieve
        results from the thought'. Effective
        management implies a high level of ability
        to act, to get things done and to make
        things happen. This ability to act
        requires not only knowledge but also high
        levels of skill. Some of these skills
        will be interpersonal (involving
        interactions with other people). Other
        skills may be more intellectual, for
        example, the analytical aspect of problem
        solving (which may also have an important
        interpersonal component);

(b)   helping managers/supervisors to develop
        interpersonal skills in their
        subordinates. This sort of activity is
        often referred to as 'coaching', but
        rarely includes any elements of
        interpersonal skill development.

These comments also apply to other professional
people, e.g. negotiators, sales representatives,
doctors, advocates, etc..

The view taken in this monograph is that
interpersonal skill development should result in
new behaviours, in which people have confidence,
being added to their existing repertoires.

SUMMARY

The basic assumptions underlying this monograph are

that the interpersonal skills to be developed are
work related, and that such development is to be
facilitated by a trainer, teacher, manager or
supervisor (facilitator). The monograph is
intended as a guide to facilitators and includes
three elements, theory, practice and
self-development activity. There are a number of
dilemmas and problems with 'traditional' approaches
to behavioural skill development which will be
confronted and solutions suggested. There is
considerable relevance to management development
both in the role of learner and of coach, but many
of the principles apply to other professionals
people.

2 Developing skills

Defining the different types of learning
outcome. The particular problems in skill
development. Holistic, atomistic and
composite learning. Goals and outcomes and
the gaps in between.

LEARNING OUTCOMES

During a lifetime people experience many different
forms of learning. They will learn different
things in different ways and if they do not suffer
major deterioration of their brain, learning can
extend for the whole lifetime. This does not deny
ideas that people may have a dominant or preferred
learning style, a concept developed by Kolb and
Fry, and Mumford and Honey (Kolb and Fry, 1976)
(Mumford and Honey 1982). It should be remembered,
however, that Kolb and Fry's research and
publication were 'Towards an applied theory of
experiential learning'. Their now famous cycle
does not include learning from 'teaching' or
trainer 'inputs', thus excluding a major stimulus
to learning. Although a learner may have a

7

dominant style, s(he) may still learn different things in different ways. For example, the way I learned to ride a bicycle was different from the way I learned calculus. This supports the idea of creating different learning proceses for different types of learning outcomes, which will be dealt with in Chapter 7.

Much that we learn occurs through 'natural' processes which in some cases may also be unconscious. In other cases learning will be deliberately facilitated. This raises the interesting question 'Is there any difference between natural (unaided) learning and facilitated learning?' Stuart argues that in facilitated learning there is advantage in making it as natural as possible (Stuart, 1984).

Much attention will be paid to processes of learning in subsequent Chapters, but first it is necessary to define the nature of the learning required.

Learning, or rather the outcomes of learning, can be classified into three types. In the world of industrial and commercial training this classification is often cited as

Knowledge
Skill
Attitude

In a more academic setting Bloom et al. have produced vast 'taxonomies of educational objectives in the cognitive and affective domain' (Bloom, 1971 and 1972). The taxonomy on skill is conspicuous by its absence. This, however, gives us another trio of learning outcomes viz.:

Cognitive
Skill
Affective

In the context of training and development relating to a work situation these are often equated to simpler words least they appear too 'academic' viz:

```
Cognitive = knowing
Skill = doing
Affective = feeling
```

The fitting of specific learning outcomes into these categories is, however, somewhat problematic.

COGNITIVE LEARNING

The easiest place to start is cognitive learning. Bloom et al. produced a taxonomy which differentiated various levels of learning, simple to complex. They, however, talk about developing intellectual skills which begins to blurr the differentiation between 'cognitive' and 'skill'. A great deal of learning required in the context of work is cognitive, and different levels are apparent even if this differentiation is not carried to the sophistication of the Bloom taxonomy. For example, it is generally clear whether the learning desired is at the level of specific facts or information, generalisable principles, theories, etc.

Cognitive learning is probably the type most people associate with facilitated learning, and the education process in general. Research we did some time ago on a wide range of management education, training and development activities indicated a huge bias towards cognitive learning, even though this was not always the intention (Binsted and Snell, 1981). I am making the assumption that familiarity with this type of learning outcome allows me to move on to another. This in no way is meant to suggest that cognitive learning is not important nor that enough is understood about how to facilitate it.

AFFECTIVE LEARNING

The next type I should like to examine is 'affective' learning. Here the interpretation given by Bloom is very different to that commonly used in the context of training and education for work. The Bloom taxonomy contains such items as 'a willingness to respond' and 'organisation of a value system'. The classification by Thayer and Beeler seems much more appropriate to the world of work and perhaps the management and supervisory aspects in particular (Thayer and Beeler, 1976). They suggest such learning outcomes as 'self awareness, exposure of feelings, accepting others values, etc.'. To these I would add outcomes familiar to people working in the Organisational Development field. Such things as getting in touch with one's feelings, handling emotional data, giving and receiving feedback in sensitive areas etc.

It is perhaps important at this stage to distinguish between having feelings, talking about feelings, or thinking about feelings. None of these necessarily result in affective learning. From the research already alluded to, we found very little evidence of affective learning in the sample of management and supervisory activities we looked at, and only then, when associated with certain very specific types of learning process. One reason why we found it difficult to find examples was that few of the sessions we video-taped had any affective learning goals. Another was the highly skilled and to some extent unorthodox interventions needed to facilitate such learning. Another factor seems to be the belief that affect has little to do with (Cognitive?) learning. In an early piece of research (Binsted, 1977), I asked a quite eminent professor how he dealt with emotional reactions from his students. He informed me that the situation never arose because he did not teach an emotional subject. Others would, of course hotly dispute this and argue that any learning is an emotional experience (Cantor, 1956).

In summary, affective learning in practice appears more difficult to define and achieve and its importance or even existence may be denied. In this monograph I shall be taking affective learning in a work context to be in line with the definitions offered by Thayer and common to the O.D. sphere of activity.

SKILL DEVELOPMENT

This now leaves the most problematical, definition

of learning outcome, i.e. 'skill'. In the context
of work, three sub-categories of skill seem
appropriate as follows.

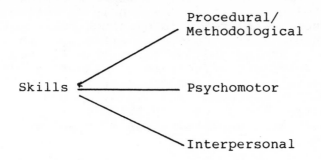

'Procedural/Methodological' will include
techniques, problem solving models etc., examples
are such things as learning how to diagnose faults
using a fault finding routine or drawing a critical
path schedule.

'Psychomotor' includes manual skills.

'Interpersonal' includes all skills involving
interaction with others, verbal skills, etc..

When considering how to facilitate learning of
these different types of skill, certain affinities
are apparent, which can be shown in Figure 2.1.

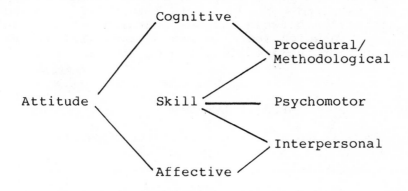

Figure 2.1 Affinities of Learning Categories

11

Procedural/methodological skills have an affinity with cognitive learning. This affinity suggests that for learning to occur we need facilitation which is effective in the cognitive learning area, together with facilitation which is effective in the skill development area. In distinction, interpersonal skills have most affinity with affective learning and facilitation will need elements which are effective for affective learning and elements which are effective for skill development. Psychomotor skill are shown as having no affinities though one can think of situations which could include either cognitive and or affective.

The model in Figure 2.1 though simplistic does give the opportunity to fit 'attitude' in. Attitudinal learning in the work context seems always to mean 'changing attitudes', to be more helpful, to increase motivation or acceptance, or to construe new situations, or factors in a problem. Attitude change has affinity with both cognitive and affective learning, and related concepts like 'values' would seem to have both thought-through as well as emotional elements.

In the context of work, learning is often linked with some defined behaviour change. Indeed the behaviour change is often the sole reason for investing in learning activities. To get a required change in behaviour, learning of more than one type may be required. The model in Figure 2.1 is based on affinities between various learning outcomes and the ways in which learning can be facilitated. We now consider the specification of the learning outcomes.

HOLISTIC AND COMPOSITE LEARNING

I would like to differentiate between the two in a way which some may find controversial.

Holistic learning stems from the idea that different categories of learning proceed together and are inextricably mixed into a total experience.

As Cantor affirms 'to learn is to change'. Also that any learning is an emotional experience (Cantor, 1956). A number of eminent educationalists subscribe to this view. The implications of this is that any learning activity should not pose restraints which would inhibit this process. More positively the facilitator should design activities which will encourage holistic learning.

Composite learning acknowledges that there may be elements of learning which fall into different categories. Thus to establish new behaviour there may be elements of cognitive learning, skill development and attitude change. Two examples might clarify this point.

Example 1, the behaviour required is that an apprentice fitter should be able to sharpen a cutting tool on a power grindstone. There will be cognitive elements like knowing the cutting face profile and angle required. There will be a psychomotor skill involved in guiding and holding the tool. An affective element may be getting over initial fears of putting two hands close to a high speed grinding wheel or the fear that the tool will jump. Attitude change may be needed about wearing safety goggles during the operation.

Example 2, the behaviour required is that a computer salesman should be better able to deal with customers who complain of late delivery. There could be cognitive elements like knowing the technical details about production or testing difficulties. Interpersonal skill elements such as convincing the customer that he (the salesman) has heard and understood the consequences of the customer's complaint and the effect on his business. Affective elements might be getting to grips with the salesman's anxiety about losing the next order, because he is still short on his sales target. Another aspect of such a situation could be an attitudinal element where the salesman might have a view that 'the customer has every incentive to buy elsewhere and it would serve that shower in production right if he did'.

It must be emphasised that holistic and composite are not polar opposites. The opposite of holistic

is atomistic. This latter would suggest that the
elements of learning should be split up and
sequenced into an optimum order. I recognise
that these two views represent two very different
educational philosophies. I take the view that it
is foolish to adhere exclusively to one or the
other. The idea that some things are best learned
in sequence acknowledges the principle of
prerequisites, and ideas developed by Gagné (Gagné,
1970). Certainly skill development activities often
embody repeated practice which produces fluency.
Another useful way of describing skill development
is to recognise the four stages.

> Unconscious incompetence
> Conscious incompetence
> Conscious competence
> Unconscious competence

Ideas that divide skill development into acquiring
core skills to which can be added more sophisticated
skills is now central to much national thinking.
All of these ideas are to some extent linked to an
atomistic philosophy. This is why I suggest that
there is a need to embrace both philosophies, but
there would seem to be some case for arguing that a
complete learning experience should be as holistic
as possible.

GOALS AND OUTCOMES

All that has been said in this chapter so far
applies to both goals (objectives) and outcomes.
The difference, as I am sure all will know, is the
difference between what learners are intended to
learn as opposed to what they actually do learn.
Again from previous research there may be yawning
gaps between the two. One noticeable feature of
this research was not so much that learning
outcomes were in a different direction from the
goals, but that they fell short of the goals. This
was particularly the case in the interpersonal
skills area. For example learners may have become
more aware of what skilled behaviour looked like,
but had not developed the ability to behave
differently. That was one of the better sort of
outcomes. Learning (as recorded by the learner)

often degenerated into rather low level cognitive learning. The thing I dread most on any interpersonal skill workshop I run is, when a learner, in answer to the question 'What did you learn?' replies 'that it is difficult'.

One reason why outcomes may not match goals is that the goals have not been set properly either by the facilitator or the learner or both. I find it helpful to distinguish between 'Action Goals' and 'Learning Goals'.

Action Goals describe what learners are expected to do in the broadest sense. These are often referred to as behavioural objectives. As important, but more difficult to define are the Learning Goals which answer the question 'what do you have to learn to be able to do what is required'. The two sorts of goal are clearly linked and are both prerequisites for designing any learning activity. The process can be shown diagrammatically in Figure 2.2.

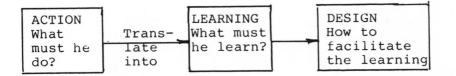

Figure 2.2 Developing Learning Goals

The translation of action goals into learning goals is I believe, the most difficult stage in the whole process of designing learning activities. Nowhere is this more so than in the area of interpersonal skills. The next chapter will suggest how this problem can be solved.

SUMMARY

There are three types of learning, cognitive, affective and skill development. In practice learning outcomes can be fitted into these types, but the boundaries between them can be blurred.

Skills are particularly problematical. People learn different things in different ways. Procedural/methodological skills learning have an affinity with cognitive learning. Interpersonal skill learning has an affinity with affective learning. Holistic learning ideas draw attention to the total nature of learning as an emotional experience. Atomistic learning ideas stress breaking down learning in related parts with sequencing from simple to difficult. Both can be utilised although a total learning experience should be holistic. Learning may often be composite, i.e. combinations of cognitive/skill/ affective/attitudinal. Goals and outcomes may often be at variance especially in the field of interpersonal skills. Action goals need to be translated into learning goals.

3 Defining interpersonal skills

What skills are, and a 3 level method of
defining them. Some practical difficulties.
Levels at which learning has to take place.

In the previous chapter I emphasised the difference
between action goals and learning goals and the
particular difficulty there was in defining goals
(which hopefully will be translated into outcomes)
for interpersonal skill development.

DEFINITIONS OF SKILL

By far the most satisfactory definition of skill I
have found is by Argyris and Schon. Their
definition is.

> Skills are dimensions of ability to behave
> effectively in situations of action. (Argyris
> and Schon, 1976.)

This definition is useful in two ways, first it
indicates what skills are, i.e. dimensions of

ability. If we think of a dimension as in Figure
3.1, high ability is associated with effective
behaviours and low ability with ineffective
behaviour.

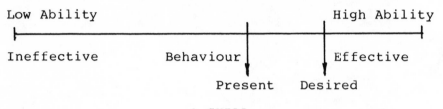

Dimensions of Ability

A SKILL

Figure 3.1

    Any effective behaviour may be composed of
numerous 'dimensions of ability' or skills, as will
be demonstrated a little further on in this chapter.
With experienced people they will already have
some level of ability, and skill development
activities will be aimed at 'moving them up the
dimension'. In general people already have some
levels of interpersonal skill (dimensions of
ability) and training does not start at no ability.

    The second way in which this definition is useful
is as a way of defining skills with a precision
which greatly helps in subsequent development. It
suggests 3 levels of definition which are carried
out in the opposite sequence to the order in the
definition itself.

A 3 level method of accurately defining
interpersonal skill

Level 1 involves defining the 'situation of action'
by defining the activity and the context in which
it occurs.

    For example, a manager may have a particular need
to make a presentation of a new idea to her board
of directors. The first step in the definition of
the skills required is to define the 'situation of

18

action'. In this case 'to make a presentation of my ideas to the Board at one of their regular meetings'.

This is a step which is often missed out and as a result skills are often only defined in portmanteau terms, such as 'presentation skills'. Clearly what the learner needs to do to succeed with her Board of Directors is likely to be very different if she was presenting unpalatable facts to her shop stewards, although both are subsumed under the generic heading of presentation skills. Each element of the 'situation of action' is important. They are her ideas (high ownership), it is the Board (her superiors, who will say yes or no) it is at their regular meeting (other items on the agenda). Defining the situation of action gives context, and begins to help experienced people to visualise the situation. This is the first essential step in skill definition.

Level 2 is to define what to 'behave effectively' means. Using our example of the manager requiring to make a presentation to her Board this second stage requires definition of what an effective presentation would be. Under these circumstances, there may be a number of different aspects of effectiveness which need definition. In this example an effective behaviour could be defined by the manager as 'to make a presentation in such a way as to':

(a)   get their ownership of the ideas (by internalising);
(b)   increase my credibility;
(c)   get them to make a decision.

This second level of definition is more difficult to get right, and in some instances may be controversial. For example, in a selection interviewing situation one learner may feel that the effective behaviour in a particular situation is to first put the interviewee at ease to get them to open up, whereas another person may feel that it is better to put them under pressure and see how they cope. More will be said about this in the next chapter. Clearly, however, the dimensions of ability (skill) involved will be quite different

depending which behaviour is thought to be
effective.

Level 3, is to define the 'dimensions of ability'.
This is by far the most difficult stage of the
process. There may be a number of dimensions many
of which may not have been identified in any
precise way before. In our example, the
'dimensions of ability' for making a presentation
which 'increased her credibility with her Board of
Directors' might include:

(a)   using their words and language;
(b)   indicating deep understanding or grasp of
        the problem or issue;
(c)   seeing things from their perspective;
(d)   being assertively confronting;
(e)   not projecting her own anxiety or
        nervousness in the situation;
(f)   adopting the optimum level of sapiential
        authority without 'blinding them with
        science';
(g)   giving signals for managing the process;
(h)   negotiating adequate space in the air-time
        available;
(i)   using visual aids;
(j)   getting the sequence right;
(k)   listening to their questions and comments
        and demonstrating understanding of their
        point.

Such skill might well contribute to the other two
effective behaviours.

This level of definition is still more difficult
in practice. It may stem from research or writing,
or some types of behaviour analysis. Definition
may be based on past successful experience of people
in a group, or be entirely intuitive. Whatever the
source of definition one problem is how to
articulate it so that the learner can comprehend it.
An example may help to clarify this point.
Consider the situation where two learners have just
completed an interview as a role play. Feedback to
the interviewer is that he should be more empathic.
Everybody agrees including the interviewer; but he
has a problem. What exactly does he have to do
differently to be more empathic, after all that was

what he was trying to be? If the learning process
is left at this stage the learner is stuck, because
the message he has got is that he has low ability
at being empathic but has no idea how to improve
the situation. If the process stops at this point
it is not a skill development activity at all. In
fact it could have a negative effect in that the
learner has now lost confidence in his ability to
be empathic. In such a situation it may be that no
one in the group can articulate the required
dimensions of ability. What some members of the
group may be able to do is demonstrate higher
abilities at being empathic, and by seeing these
more effective empathic behaviours, then it will be
quite easy to appreciate what the dimensions of
ability actually are. For example, a third level
definition of a dimension of ability to produce
empathy could be 'to identify with some of the
interviewee's experience', 'yeah, I wasn't too clear
what I wanted to do when I took my first job
either'. It is at this third level of definition
that learning needs to take place. It is quite
usual in some skill development situations that the
third level of definition (dimensions of ability)
cannot be articulated by either group or trainer at
the beginning of a session.

LEVEL OF LEARNING

The question the foregoing raises is 'how does the
definition of skills help the design and running of
interpersonal skill development activities?'
Reference has already been made to the need to
translate action goals into learning goals. The
three stage process of definition just described
does this quite well. Level 1 and 2 define the
action goals and Level 3 defines the learning
goals.

    If skills are only defined as very general
portmanteau skills (which can hardly be called
definitions), e.g. 'communication skills', there is
no real focus for learning. If they are defined in
a much more precise way based on the Argyris and
Schon definition, then at least learning goals are
identified at the right level. People's ability to
act more effectively is unlikely to be improved

unless learning involves working with 'dimensions of ability' (Level 3). Shaw makes a similar point in respect of training for selling skills. He defines the levels as behavioural strategies, skills and tactics. He emphasises the need to work at all 3 levels (Shaw, 1981).

In practice, management training events often appear to define skills so vaguely that skill development activities are correspondingly unfocused and ineffective from the client's point of view. In this monograph, I shall be dealing with ways of developing specific accurately defined skills which are focused sufficiently for effective learning to result.

This, however, produces somewhat of a paradox because as has already been seen, the level at which learning needs to take place is just the level at which it is so difficult to define goals. This, in practice, causes no great problem providing designs and facilitation recognise this situation. In practice this means that the learner group must work at the third level of definition for true skill development to occur, but it is not essential for dimensions of ability to be articulated before the session starts, although this must occur at some point during the learning process. There is generally a tendency for the group to work more easily at Level 2, and although this can be productive working at this level only, does not in general achieve development of abilities. The practical outworking of this principle will be dealt with in Chapter 7 and onwards.

SUMMARY

The Argyris and Schon definition of skills first emphasises that skills are dimensions (of ability) and second, provides a 3 level method of definition. Level 1 defines the context, Level 2 defines the effective behaviour and Level 3 the skill (dimension of ability). The latter is the most difficult to define and articulate. It may not be possible to do this without first seeing skilled behaviour and then analysing what made it skilled. Learning has to occur at the 3rd Level of definition for real skill development to occur.

4 Skill development

It is now an appropriate time to try and put some
of the content of Chapter 3 into practice. This
chapter is designed to help you explore practical
situations and draw your own conclusions. The
focus will be on defining skills using the three
level approach. A number of different activities
are offered, there is a logic in their order, but
of course you may wish to leave some out. Some
practice at this point is, however, recommended.

MENU OF ACTIVITIES

Activity 1, this involves reading a short
description of an interaction and then carrying out
an analysis. Your analysis can be compared with
some observations actually made when the
interaction was taking place.

Activity 2, this involves generating your own
short example and doing an analysis.

Activity 3, involves using a video or training
film to which you have access for use as a basis

for analysis.

Activity 4, involves going out with a video
camera and recording a 15 minute interaction
between a small number of people as a basis for
analysis.

Activity 5, involves sitting in on live
interaction and noting and analysing the dimensions
of ability being used.

   The activities are arranged in increasing order
of difficulty.   Full directions are given with each
one.

   This chapter is arranged in work-page form so
that you can refer to your own work at later stages
in the book.

ACTIVITY 1 IDENTIFYING SKILLS FROM AN EXAMPLE

Process

1. Read the short description of an interaction.
2. Describe the 'situation of action'.
3. List some 'effective behaviours' that could be used.
4. Identify some 'dimensions of ability'.
5. Compare with the list on p. 30.

1. Description of an interaction

A sales engineer is in the middle of a quite successful interview with a customer who he knows well and with whom he considers he has a good relationship. The sales engineer is proceeding confidently with the interview (which so far is going according to his plan), when the customer brings up an issue of poor performance of a piece of equipment that the sales engineer has sold to him. The customer is a sub-contractor and on installing the equipment in the final customer's premises, found that he had to do a considerable amount of remedial work to get the installation operational. He points out to the sales engineer with some force that this has been very costly, and since the sales engineer's organisation is large and flourishing and he is a small businessman running a sub-contracting business, that he should be compensated for the time and effort which he has had to put in to get the installation operational. He becomes rather angry, and quite carried away with his arguments, and the justice of his claim and demands to know what the sales engineer is going to do about it. The sales engineer who is clearly good at thinking quickly 'on his feet' begins to reason with the customer and to agree some action that he will take, being careful to do certain things and avoid doing others.

His dilemma is that he does not want to foul up the deal he still hopes to make, to sell more new equipment (he is a bit behind his sales targets). On the other hand he does not want to land his company with an obligation to pay compensation.

2. List the key elements in this 'situation of action'

3. Now make a list of 'effective behaviours' that the sales engineer could have used

4. Identifying dimensions of ability

Now take two or three of your 'effective
behaviours' and identify the dimensions of ability
that are appropriate for each effective behaviour.
You may find this difficult, so try to visualise
the interaction, and think how you would behave in
a similar situation. The purpose of this activity
is not to get right answers, but to experiment with
the process.

5. Comparison

Compare what you have written with some observations actually made during the interaction described. These you will find on page 30. Please note these may differ to some degree from yours, but this does not signify rightness or wrongness. Only experimentation in the same situation with the same person could begin to establish that. The point of this activity is to help you identify and distinguish the three levels of skill definition. Have another think about it, try a few more ideas which might work in the given example. You may find it helpful to re-read Chapter 3, make a few notes and then try another activity.

End of Activity 1.

OBSERVATIONS ACTUALLY MADE IN THE SITUATION
DESCRIBED IN SELF DEVELOPMENT ACTIVITY 1

1. Some key elements in the 'situation of
    action'.

    (a) There is a good relationship with the
        customer. The sales engineer has some
        'credit'.
    (b) The sales engineer has a plan for the
        interview.
    (c) The customer got angry and was reinforcing
        belief in the justice of the case.
    (d) The customer demands action.
    (e) The sales engineer wants the new order
        badly.

2. Some 'effective behaviours' that the sales
    engineer might use.

    (a) Avoids admitting that the company is in
        default.
    (b) Avoids saying anything that could be
        construed as a promise of compensation.
    (c) Tries to cool the customer down.
    (d) Indicates that he has understood the
        complaint and its effect on the customer's
        business.
    (e) Sympathises with the customer's dilemma.
    (f) Offers and agrees some action, so he can
        continue the interaction and press the
        current sale.

   You may find yourself disagreeing with some or
all of these. This is not unusual. Views of these
issues may not be based on sound research, but on
some combination of opinion, personal and
organisational norms and values, or past experience
or observation. Since some of these are unique to
any individual, some disagreement seems inevitable.
How such disagreement can be dealt with is covered
in Chapter 5.

3. Some abilities that the sales engineer might
    need:

    (i) to cool the customer down 2 (c):

-   not to show signs of irritation by change in voice pitch, body posture, etc.;
-   keep cool out of an adult ego state with expressions such as 'how many hours did it take to put things right?' (Harris, 1969);
-   do not refute his statements, but explore their validity;
-   keep his cool.

(ii) to indicate understanding 2 (d).

-   ask questions of clarification which demonstrate understanding;
-   give signals that he is still tuned in 'ugh-hugh', 'yeh', nodding etc.;
-   play back what the customer has said, accurately!
-   complete the customer's argument;
-   summarise;
-   suggest implications,
-   positively indicate understanding, 'right, got it', 'yes, I can see the problem'.

Again these suggestions may be different from yours. The point is are they at the same level (3) as yours? If not see if you can think up some more.

ACTIVITY 2 IDENTIFYING SKILLS FROM YOUR EXPERIENCE

Process

1. Generate a description of an interaction from your experience.
2. Describe the situation of action.
3. List some effective behaviours.
4. Identify some dimensions of ability.
5. Reflect on the process.

1. Generating the description

Think of a situation from your experience which you felt you handled rather well. It should be an interaction between two or more people, you being a key person in this. Thus it could be a 1 to 1 interaction (like you giving some feedback to a subordinate, which was being rejected) or a 1 to group (like you giving some bad news to three other people). Recall what happened as accurately as possible and then write it below.

Description

2. List key elements in the 'situation of action'

3. Now make a list of the behaviours you used which helped to make the interaction effective

4. As before take two or three of the effective
behaviours and identify the 'dimensions of ability'
which are appropriate to each. The purpose of this
element of the activity is to help you to identify
dimensions of ability which you use.

5. Reflection

Think about the process you have just been through.
Can you spot any differences between this thinking
through of something in your experience and the
previous use of an example (which might have been
remote from your experience)? Does it say anything
about your preference for using your own experience
to using a case study? Have you really got down to
level 3 this time? You might like to jot down any
ideas you have.

End of Activity 2

ACTIVITY 3 IDENTIFYING SKILLS FROM VIDEO OR FILM

Process

1. View the video or film sequence.
2. Pick out the key elements of the 'situation of action'.
3. Pick out those behaviours which are effective and those which are not.
4. Identify dimensions of ability associated with the effective behaviours, and specify which abilities would have made the ineffective behaviours effective.
5. Reflections.

Introduction

In this activity you will be moving from contemplating descriptions or recall of interactions to observing from an audio-visual record of some interaction. Since it is recorded the interaction may be viewed several times, which makes it much easier to do the analysis than if it is all done in real time. Activity 5 requires real time analysis, which is an important skill for the trainer to develop. If you are handling a training session using video it is often possible to, as it were, get two 'goes' at analysis, the first time live the second time recorded. In doing this third activity it is a good idea to minimise the number of viewings at first and then review to check accuracy. The process suggested is based on these notions.

1. Viewing the video or film sequence

The first thing to do is to select an appropriate sequence from any material available to you. Something of 10 minutes' duration or less should be adequate. More important, the quality needs to be right. It will be important for the behaviour to be effective rather than neutral and definitely not predominantly ineffective. A mixture would be satisfactory but a 'how not to do it' sequence should be avoided. In the interpersonal skill area 'how not to do it' sequences often seem to predominate, thus focusing learning on behaviour to avoid. Although such learning can be both

memorable and useful, there are often more serious
negative consequences which will be referred to in
subsequent chapters. For the purpose of this
activity, analysis of effective behaviour will
predominate although some ineffective behaviour may
be included. The sequences may be acted or live
documentary, or recordings of sessions you have
taped, or recording off air. View the sequence
once only before doing the next two elements of the
activity. Look out for the key elements in the
situation and the effective behaviours.

2. Pick out the key elements in the 'situation of action'

3. List the effective and ineffective behaviours you observed

Effective behaviours

Ineffective behaviours

4. Now identify the dimensions of ability which are
present in the effective behaviours. Then describe
the ones which are missing from the ineffective
behaviours. Try and do this without a further
viewing, then view again to check your first
observations. Add to your list and view again if
useful. Continue this until you feel you have
captured all the dimensions of ability. If you
find it difficult to find any, this could be
because the behaviour is neutral and not very
effective or clear cut. In this event try another
sequence.

**Dimensions of ability associated with effective
behaviour**

Dimensions of ability missing from ineffective behaviour

5. Think about the process you have just been
through. Did you find the observation difficult?
Did you need to view several times? If you need
less viewing in the next activity you are showing
signs of developing your skill of spotting the
'dimensions of ability'. Did you find it easier or
more difficult to observe what was there or to
speculate on what was missing? Why do you think
this was so? Jot down any ideas you have.

End of Activity 3

ACTIVITY 4 IDENTIFYING SKILL FROM AN INTERACTION
YOU HAVE VIDEO-RECORDED

Process

1. Decide on the key elements of the 'situation of action'.
2. Set up and make a short video-recording of a suitable interaction.
3. Pick out effective and ineffective behaviours.
4. Identify dimensions of ability.
5. Reflections.

Introduction

This activity has similarities with activity 3 since it involves analysis from a recorded interaction. There are, however, some significant differences which will be highlighted. In doing this activity it will be useful to consciously build on activity 3.

1. Decide on the key elements of the situation of action you wish to create or capture on video. Note them down. This obviously will need to be feasible in terms of what you can set up.

As an alternative you may wish to capture a live situation which may or may not prove to be a good sample to work from, e.g. a real manager doing a real interview. It will undoubtedly offer an interesting learning situation. If you do this, listing the elements of the situation of action will be a second operation.

2. Setting up and making the video

This offers a number of different options compared with using a sequence already available. For example, it can be made in the area you are most concerned about, can be set up very informally with colleagues, can be of not particularly high technical standard, can last about 15 minutes, etc.. It will be important to set up an effective interaction where (as in activity 3) effective behaviour predominates over ineffective. While setting up and recording the interaction, the opportunity can be taken to do a first attempt at a live analysis. At this point (if you have done all the other Activities so far), you should be familiar with the different levels at which you are searching for data.

It is also a good idea to index the tape as you go along, if you are using a fixed camera. The important thing is to give a clear succint briefing to those to be involved, avoiding over briefing and role playing.

The trick is to get them to take roles. Thus a briefing might go along these lines, assuming a one-to-one interaction.

> Thanks for coming along for half an hour, I want to set up an interviewing situation where a boss is trying to give a subordinate some slightly critical feedback about performance. The problem is the subordinate is rejecting and denying the feedback and the assessment procedure, as you know full well, requires that she signs the form saying you both agree the assessment. I've got two copies of our standard form with comments about one area of performance. You know the general procedure. Read the comments on the form and when you are

ready, Fred would you like to be the boss and talk to Liz who can be the subordinate. I don't want you to role play. Do it how you would normally do it. When you are ready give me a shout and I will start to tape the interaction. Arrange the desk and chairs as you like. Any problems?

   This quick setting up of what I call 'instant case studies' is dealt with in much more detail in Chapter 8.

3. List the effective and ineffective behaviours observed

Effective Behaviours

Ineffective behaviours

4. Identify the dimensions of ability

Now identify the dimensions of ability which are
present in the effective behaviours. Then describe
the ones which could have made the ineffective
behaviours into effective ones. If you have used a
fixed camera try a first analysis without looking
at the recording. If busy with the camera you will
almost certainly need to look at the recording
before you start listing. As in activity 3
review and fill in the picture as often as you
feel necessary.

Dimensions of ability associated with effective behaviour

Dimensions of ability missing from ineffective behaviour

5. Think about the process you have just been
through. Have a look at the dimensions of ability
you have identified in the other activities. Are
you getting a feel for 'level 3' definitions of
skills? As you will see later, the ability to
recognise learning at level 3 is vital to this
approach. You may find it useful to jot down any
thoughts you have.

End of activity 4.

ACTIVITY 5 IDENTIFYING SKILL IN A LIVE INTERACTION

Process

1. Arrange to sit in on some interaction.
2. Without getting involved yourself, analyse down to level 3 taking as many rough notes as you can.
3. Sort out the analysis and record.
4. Reflection.

Introduction

This activity gives a one-off opportunity to analyse an interaction without the aid of a video recording. It all has to stem from direct observation. This will often be the position a trainer or manager (facilitator) may find themselves in when training or coaching. This real time analysis is the most difficult to do, and involves making immediate judgements about effective behaviour as well as what was it that made it effective/ineffective.

1. Choose an interaction that you are interested in and negotiate to be a 'fly on the wall', i.e. not to get involved. The principle here is to avoid influencing the interaction in any way. This is sometimes quite difficult to avoid, but taking simple precautions like sitting outside the interaction, and out of anyone's sight line greatly helps. It can also be very helpful to clarify your role during the interaction.

2. Make notes as the interaction proceeds and look out for the three levels of data. It is very useful to capture key phrases verbatim. An example might be, in a selection interview situation, the interviewer might say 'obviously we want to see if you will suit our needs, but it is equally important that you find out if the job will suit you'. This may be seen as a helpful contribution to setting a friendly and relaxed climate or clarifying roles in the interview (an effective behaviour).

3. Analyse from the notes and recall, using the
same pattern as for activity 3 and 4.

(a) List the key elements in the situation of
action

(b) List the effective and ineffective behaviours
observed

Effective Behaviours

Ineffective behaviours

(c) As before identify dimensions of ability
present and absent, and this time associate with
the key phrases used.

Dimensions of ability associated with effective
behaviour

Dimensions of ability missing from ineffective behaviour

4. Reflect on all the work done so far.

Which were the most difficult activities or parts of activities from your experience? Can you think of a reason for this? If there are any residual problems try reading Chapter 3 again or repeat the activities you found most difficult, using different examples. Again you may like to make notes to summarise any conclusions or ideas you have.

End of Activity 5.

5 Strategies for developing interpersonal skills

The process of developing skills, awareness
raising and the ability to act. Ways of
establishing dimensions of ability.

Having examined a way of defining interpersonal
skills of the more complex kind, which are
appropriate to management, supervisory and
professional development, this Chapter considers
the question of how such skills can be learned.
First there is the question of the development
process. There are two quite easily discernible
stages in the process of developing interpersonal
skills.

RAISING AWARENESS

This is all about recognising what skilled
behaviour looks like, e.g. what it is that makes a
good presentation compared with a poor one, or an
empathic interview compared with an abrasive one.
In essence (using the Argyris and Schon definition)
this recognition makes people aware of the

dimensions of ability associated with an effective behaviour in the context of a situation of action.

As you will already have discovered, from the self development activities, recognising the dimensions of ability and making a judgement about what degree of ability a person is exhibiting in an interaction, is not easy. It is not even clear on occasions what constitutes effective behaviour. If you look back at your notes on the activities in Chapter 4, you may notice a difference in those cases where you had to imagine or speculate (activity 1 and 2), and those where you could observe, especially when you could do the latter several times (using a video replay). You were observing other people's abilities or lack of them, which resulted in awareness of skills (dimensions of ability).

A further and even more important aspect of awareness is to recognise the characteristics of one's own behaviour, and its effect on others. When awareness is about one's own skills, this can either be positive or negative. In a work situation it is often the case that there is no illumination of the level of one's skills. There may be total absence of any feedback. This means that awareness is not raised, and hence no learning or development will take place. This may be due to any number of reasons. For example, a subordinate may recognise that the way his boss always seems to 'put people down' antagonises them, and makes people avoid contact with him unless summoned. As a subordinate he will have experienced negative feelings about this on many occasions. But how can he say anything to raise the bosses awareness? He may find it difficult to articulate meaningful feedback, or feel that it would be far to risky to attempt to do so (that would surely invite a 'put down' to beat all others). Another example could be when a manager is interviewing someone for a job and is intending to be relaxed and informal but in reality is experienced by the interviewee as abrasive. In the normal course of such an interview (particularly if it is a one-to-one) the manager is unlikely to become aware of how his behaviour is experienced by the interviewee. The difficulties of raising awareness in the work situation are of course one reason why specially designed skill development activities are such an important area of training and education. In a training situation one key component which can be provided is feedback specifically aimed at raising awareness.

Negative Awareness

One way in which awareness can be raised is in a negative sense. This in effect informs the learner of things they cannot do, or not do very well (low levels of ability). This sort of awareness raising is often a necessary component of learning, but severe problems arise if this is the only form of learning to take place. No trainer would suggest that this was a desirable situation because the predictable consequence for the learner would be loss of self esteem and confidence, and feeling of frustration that they did not know what to do about it. Nevertheless, some traditional designs may on occasions result in this happening, and this may be compounded by trainers' attitudes towards how trainers can best facilitate skill learning.

I have found one attitude quite prevalent among trainers. This is that people learn best from their mistakes. One such design for learning is to set up some situation or activity which the learners are required to perform, the expectation being that this will show up a number of deficiencies in their interpersonal skills. These deficiencies can then be fed back and form the basis of a debriefing session when the learners are expected to learn how to do it 'properly' or 'better' in the future. I have heard the view expressed that the worst thing that can happen in a skill development activity is if somebody makes a superlative job of the task in hand, and the trainer therefore is unable to point out any shortcomings. One outcome of this thinking is to design tasks for learners which are so difficult that there is very little chance of them performing well. This may give the trainer a feeling of security because there will be plenty of problems to discuss. Two examples may perhaps illustrate the sort of outcomes of such approaches and thinking.

The first I am ashamed to admit is from my own experience, and concerns a workshop I ran (with others) for staff committee members. The object of the training was to help them to put their case firmly to, and to gently confront, senior management. We therefore set up a situation where the learners prepared a case and presented it to the trainers, who put themselves in the role of senior management. The whole session was video taped for later play back and analysis. In the event the group worked well, produced a good plan of how to make their presentation and elected what appeared to be the most capable person to take the lead. At the appointed hour the presentation was made to the 'senior management', the only difficulty being that the person who made the presentation succeeded in doing almost the opposite of all the things that had been agreed previously, the result being quite disastrous. There was then a break for dinner, and after dinner we duly showed the video play back which proved to be a source of great entertainment and hilarity to all the group except the person who had taken the lead. This left the trainers with the dilemma of what to do next and due to the late hour, helpful advice was given and the next morning we moved on to something else. The effect on the presenter I fear was strongly negative in that any confidence that he might have had was destroyed, and most of <u>his</u> learning was associated with what <u>not</u> to do.

The second example, taken from our research, was a situation in which the task given was highly complex and difficult, and during the debriefing session the predominant feeling among the group was one of frustration at not having completed the task satisfactorily. The debriefing session degenerated more and more into the trainer delivering a prolonged input to explain what they had done wrong and what might be done about it. The learning, however, was somewhat restricted (Binsted and Snell, 1982).

In both these examples awareness raising was predominately negative and although the trainers in both cases made efforts to make people aware of

52

what they _should_ have done, that was not matched with any _learning_ process.

Positive Awareness

The more satisfactory way of raising awareness is in a positive sense. This is more difficult to do in many instances. Take the example already referred to of a manager who is conducting a selection interview which he intends to be friendly and relaxed but which in reality is abrasive. Let us assume, however, that the interview has just been video taped in the context of a small group training activity where another learner has taken the role of the interviewee. Two other learners have acted as observers and the trainer has operated and indexed the video. Feedback using the video plus interviewee, observer and trainer observations will certainly highlight problems. This will raise awareness in the negative sense. Giving positive feedback about what went well will reinforce effective behaviour which is useful, but does not facilitate learning in the vital area needed. The information that his 'friendly' style is in reality rather abrasive may have come as a nasty shock, so what he now needs to become aware of is what he needs to do to correct that. This will be awareness raising in the positive sense.

This is where working at the third level of definition (based on Argyris and Schon) becomes so vital. Behavioural injunctions from, for example the trainer, like 'try and be more empathic' are of little use and only redefine the 'effective behaviour'. What the learner wants to find out is 'what do _I_ have to do or say or convey in body language to be more empathic?' As you will already have discovered in Chapter 4 describing dimensions of ability is not easy, and as far as the learner is concerned, this presents particular problems, since if he _had_ known how to be empathic in the first place he probably would have been. At the very least he must _see_ some effective empathic behaviour and be able to analyse it at level 3. In practice this means that not only must effective behaviour be _modelled_, but the learner must recognise exactly what is it that makes it effective (especially when compared with his own).

53

This sort of activity raises awareness in the positive sense.

DEVELOPING THE ABILITY TO ACT

Stage 2 of the development process is developing the ability to act. Clearly stage 1 is required to precede stage 2. From my observations and experience of training events aimed at the development of the more sophisticated interactive skills required by managers, supervisors, and professional people, many events barely reach the positive awareness raising stage, and very few stage 2. The reasons for this seem to be

(a)   trying to reach stage 2 without going through stage 1
(b)   not having adequate learning designs to facilitate stage 2 learning
(c)   stage 2 is more difficult and takes longer to achieve than stage 1.

This second stage is in every sense vital to any skill development strategy. It bridges the gap between knowing what ought to be done and being able to do it, when the occasion demands, and under the conditions that exist in the context of work. This is clearly a key element in the whole development process. In many traditional designs it may be entirely absent. In the awareness raising stage knowing what ought to be done is an important element of developing a skill, but if this is expressed in generalised and rather vague descriptive forms it leaves the learner in a dilemma. For example, injunctions like 'try and be more empathic' or 'try and identify with the customers needs a bit more' or even 'try and make the interaction more adult-adult' may not give enough insight to a learner to begin to develop more effective behaviours, hence the need to work at level 3. The learner's dilemma is that knowing what they ought to do does not mean that they know how to do it, nor that they can do it. Lastly of course whether they want to do it. The awareness raising stage should define what ought to be done, the second stage is about 'being able' to do it. In both stages it is essential to work at the

third level of definition so that the learner can
see, e.g. 'what it was John said and did that made
Sue so angry'. Again it can be said that
traditional learning designs which merely allow
for, say, role-play and feedback are unlikely to
achieve stage 1 adequately, let alone stage 2. The
theoretical reasons for this are given in the next
Chapter. The ways in which stage 2 activities can
be designed will be dealt with in some detail in
subsequent Chapters.

DEFINING THE SKILLS

So far in this Chapter we have seen the need to both
raise awareness, particularly in the positive
sense, and develop the ability to act, and in both
these stages there is a need to work at level 3 of
the Argyris and Schon definition. We still,
however, need another element to form a basis for
designing a learning event. This element is
concerned with resolving the dilemma of 'how to
establish the effective behaviours and dimensions
of ability, and the levels within those dimensions
which the learner needs to develop'.

There are three options

     1.   Research
     2.   Experience
     3.   Experiment.

It is perhaps important at this point to
emphasise that we are focusing on interpersonal
skills, where this problem is likely to be most
acute, although similar problems may exist in other
areas of skill development.

1. Research

This is an option which relies on properly
researched data about what is and what is not
effective behaviour, together with the dimension of
ability. These need defining at level 3. Some
examples are the work by Rackham and Morgan on
behaviour analysis where, for instance, effective
and ineffective group behaviours are identified.

These are concerned with group decision making
types of activity (Rackham and Morgan, 1977).

The SPIN selling skills programme offered by the
Huthwaite group is also based on extensive research
into various effective behaviours. In research
based strategies, learners develop abilities which
are known to be the elements of effective
behaviour. The restriction on the use of this
strategy is the availability of suitable research.
Credibility of the research in the learner's
perception, is also a factor especially if the
findings are counter-intuitive or in conflict with
the norms or culture of the learner's organisation.
Under these circumstances it might well be the best
option, otherwise the organisation will continue
with its sub-optimal practices.

2. Experience

In this option the experience of the learner group
is used to define effective behaviour and levels of
ability. The experience of the trainer is of
course included in this, but my personal preference
when working with a group as a trainer is to use my
own experience as a last resort. This will of
course be influenced by whether the trainer is
internal or external to the learner's organisation.
If the trainer is external and is working with a
family or cousin group who share a wealth of
factual background knowledge, and technological
jargon (e.g. like managers in the computer
industry) she may not be able to contribute very
easily. If, however, the trainer is a close
associate of the learner group (i.e. worked for
the organisation and was 'one of them' in a
previous job role), then she may be able to
contribute at a very detailed and specific level.
This has its dangers and an over enthusiasm to
contribute (trainer syndrome?) may block off
valuable contributions from learners' experience.
One very useful design for this option is to split
training into three sections. The first is an off
the job skill development activity, the second is
some field experience, where learning is tried out,
and the third is another skill development session
in which people work on their experiences gained
from their field work. This utilises 'real'

experience which is up-to-date and reflects the current situation.

3. Experiment

This option is appropriate when the dimensions of ability are not known and effective behaviour is in doubt. This can occur when for instance there is controversy and doubt about what constitutes effective behaviour, or when behaviour that was thought to be effective in the past now no longer seems to work. Another example is where new behaviour is required which no one in the group has tried before (e.g. in selling, introducing a new product or selling to a new sort of customer). In this option the group needs to develop an experimental approach and try out alternative behaviours and evaluate them within the group. This generally produces a productive and creative process and may help learners to break out of long standing areas of difficulty.

DEVELOPING THE STRATEGY

The strategy thus contains three elements

1. Raising awareness not only of what dimensions of ability are but how the learner's behaviour is seen or effects others. This needs to include positive awareness raising.

2. Developing the ability to act, which must follow from awareness raising.

3. Choosing how to define the dimensions of ability that are appropriate for the learners to develop.

What then needs to be done is to develop a learning process which will fit in with the elements of this strategy. The various elements of this will be covered in subsequent Chapters.

SUMMARY

A strategy for the design of interpersonal skill
development activities needs to cover three
elements. Awareness raising, negative, but
particularly positive aspects are required as a
first stage. Developing the ability to act is the
second stage this includes 'knowing how', 'being
able' and 'wanting to'. The third element is to do
with deciding how to find the dimensions of ability
by research, experience or experiment.

6 Basic modes of learning

The three modes of learning applied to skill development. The idea of 'whole-cycle' learning.

MODES IN GENERAL

There are three basic modes of learning which apply
to any sort of learning, whether cognitive,
affective or skill development. Some are commonly
found in some areas, but are rare in others. Both
the design of learning activities and the way in
which they are facilitated need to be quite
different for the different modes. These basic
modes of learning are:

  * Reception of inputs
  * Discovery
  * Reflection.

Examples in some areas are easy to find:

  * Reception of input may be the mode of learning
    which is operating when a learner is listening to

a lecture and making notes and may result in
cognitive learning.

* Discovery may be operating when a learner is
doing some active task and getting feedback of
the consequences and may be a way of
accomplishing skill development. (People
sometimes speak of discovering something in a
book, meaning something they did not know before.
This is not discovery, but reception of input.).

* Reflection may be the mode of learning when the
learner is gathering her thoughts together to
write an essay, and may again result in cognitive
learning.

It is quite easy to think of examples in
cognitive learning, but what are the learning
processes in the field of skill development which
correspond to the three modes?

RECEPTION OF INPUT

The essence of this mode of learning is that the
learner receives something from outside himself.
One aspect of interpersonal skill development is
the possibility of telling people how to behave
effectively or what the "dimensions of ability"
are. For example a teacher might produce the list
of the dimensions concerned with making an
effective presentation to a board of directors,
like the one in Chapter 3. The way in which people
learn what the dimensions are is more akin to
cognitive learning, in this case because the
teacher facilitates the learning by an input of
facts on a list (a strongly cognitive facilitator).
The transition to skill learning can be pinpointed
as follows.

The learner may learn from a list of 'dimensions
of ability' (again using the presentation example)
that one of these is: 'not projecting his anxiety
or nervousness into the situation'.

To know or remember that this is a dimension is
one thing, to know what he has to do, how he has to

60

behave and then to be <u>able</u> to behave effectively is
another, as we saw in Chapter 5. It is the latter
which is the true skill development part of the
learning, although the former may be an essential
pre-cursor.

A <u>skill</u> input is quite different from a cognitive
one, and involves <u>showing</u> people behaviours. This
is called demonstration or modelling, i.e.
<u>modelling or demonstrating</u> a behaviour which is
observed by the learner. This process is shown
diagrammatically in Figure 6.1.

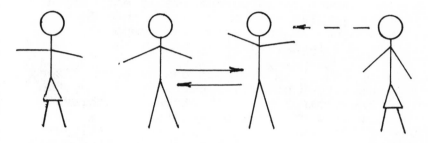

<u>Facilitator</u>   <u>Learner</u>

Sets up   Interaction   Observes

Figure 6.1 Modelling

Some practical situations in which this can occur
are.

(a) A role play in which two learners take the
     roles of manager and subordinate, and the
     manager conducts a disciplinary interview.
     This is watched live by the third learner who
     sees some behaviour which gets round a problem
     she had when doing a similar interview. This
     results in positive awareness raising and
     gives a real insight into an alternative
     behaviour which she feels she would like to
     use.
(b) A video film of how to deal with a customer
     complaint watched either by a group of
     learners or solo as a part of a distance

learning programme. In this case the film
shows the 'right way to do it'. This again
will get the learner aware of 'how to do it'.
(c) A salesman goes on a call with his boss who
takes over a difficult part of the interview
with the customer, which they will
subsequently discuss in the car. This gives
the salesman an idea about how to handle the
difficulty thus demonstrating some skills.

Shaw emphasises the need to focus learning at the
3rd level of skill definition. He puts it this way:

> Telling someone to be persuasive is not helpful
> unless persuasiveness is converted into do-able
> behaviour such as increasing the tempo of
> delivery ... (Shaw, 1981).

Learning by reception of input can be accomplished
with varying degrees of active participation by the
learners. The minimum involvement can be achieved
by using film or video tape presentation of
desirable skilled behaviour, as in example (b) just
cited. This generally implies a dependent learning
relationship (with the learner taking little or no
responsibility for any aspect of the situation) (see
Binsted and Snell, 1981). It also implies that the
maker of the film knows what skilled behaviour
includes (i.e. knows the dimensions of ability) and
is able to get someone to enact them. The net
result is a model of the right or best way to behave
in the given situation. This approach is becoming
an increasingly popular way of developing
interpersonal skills. Examples are given by Shaw
and Tosti who talk of a 'master performance' whose
quality need to be high and possibly 'customerised'
(Shaw, 1981 and Tosti 1980). At the other extreme
it is possible to explore dimensions of ability by
getting the learner group to model a variety of
behaviours and decide for themselves which are most
effective, as in example (a). This is a very
independent way of learning since the learners are
responsible for deciding what the 'dimensions' are
and which are effective. During such a process the
whole group (including the facilitator) becomes
aware of the elements of skill involved. This is

using the 'experimental' option referred to in Chapter 5. There are other options, such as a facilitator modelling high levels of skilled behaviour, but some might see this as high risk (for the facilitator.

These alternatives all rely on modelling or showing learners skilled behaviour, which can be used to identify the 'dimensions of ability' (Level 3), if these are not previously clearly defined. It is of course vital that this step is achieved. It is of limited use to demonstrate a brilliant performance if learners do not identify what it was that made it brilliant. From observations and involvement in such activities, I now hold the view that this latter part of the process is often either entirely missing or treated very superficially in the more traditional skill development activities.

Thus the key element of this mode of learning is that the learner observes a demonstration or modelling of behaviour. Its main function is to show learners alternative or new behaviours demonstrating skills they do not have (or have at an unacceptable level).

Facilitation requires setting up appropriate interactions (live or on film) and focusing attention on the Level 3 'dimensions of ability'.

Example of facilitating behaviour. The facilitator asks a member of a learner group to model some alternative behaviour for others to watch.

> "O.k. now we have discussed the presentation that Jane made to the group, and have spotted the critical bits which made Fred feel you were unsure of your facts. I wonder, Fred, if you would like to show us how you would have done it? What would you have said?"

DISCOVERY

This mode of learning is the easiest to recognise and find in the practice of skill development.

Discovery learning involves action by the learner and feedback, e.g. a learner tries out some behaviour, gets feedback on the effect and thereby learns. In the interpersonal skill area we can describe discovery learning as:

Experimentation or Practice with Feedback

Many traditional skill development activities such as role play, structured experiences etc., rely entirely on this mode of learning.

Most facilitators are well aware of the necessity of setting up appropriate situations to allow learners to generate relevant behaviour. Examples are simulation, 'here and now' interactions in small groups, role plays perhaps based on case studies, projects or using 'real life' work experiences. There is little problem in getting learners into action. What seems to be more problematical (from personal experience, observations and research) is how to generate feedback to facilitate learning. This I believe to be the key to effective discovery learning. A whole Chapter (14) is devoted to feedback strategies.

The essential element for the learner is that she must take action and get feedback about that action. The process is shown diagrammatically in Figure 6.2 and 6.3. You will note only one person is designated as 'learner' because only she is involved in the discovery process. Other learners are shown, but will be learning by different modes.

Facilitator   Learner
Sets up and   Interaction   Observing
observes

Figure 6.2 Discovery Learning: Stage 1

Facilitator   Learner

Gives and/   Gives   Gets   Give
or elicits   feedback   feedback   feedback
feedback
from the
group

Figure 6.3 Discovery Learning. Stage 2

   Some practical situations in which discovery
learning can occur.

(a)   In a triad practicing a selection interview.
      The learner is taking his real life role as
      manager, another is taking the role of the
      candidate and the third is observing, as is
      the facilitator. When the interview is
      completed the tutor elicits feedback from
      first the 'candidate' and then the 'observer'.

(b)   A learner is making a presentation to the rest
      of the group as part of a presentation skills
      workshop. The learners, as they are on the
      receiving end of the presentation, mark a
      score sheet to note the frequency of certain
      behaviour. Each focuses on a different
      aspect of behaviour, and each of these has
      been previously defined and can be recognised
      by all the members of the group. When the
      presentation is complete the tutor asks each
      member of the group to share what they have

recorded and this is discussed with the 'presenter'.

(c)   A salesman makes a visit to a customer with his boss. The salesman does nearly all of the talking, the boss saying as little as possible without appearing rude. As soon as they get back into the car the boss starts a 'kerb side coaching session' and gives the salesman feedback about how he saw the interview going.

There will be a different quality to the feedback in the various examples because in some cases it is from the person on the receiving end of the interaction (from the candidate in (a) and from the presentee in (b)).

As with the reception of input mode of learning the mode does not predispose the facilitator to create any particular level of dependence or independence of the learner. For example, the facilitator may himself give all the feedback in a very authoritative way, which will tend to create a dependant learner relationship. This will be enhanced if the feedback is both highly critical and evaluative. On the other hand if the facilitator elicits feedback from the other learners and gives no opinion himself, this will tend to create independant learners. Again it is of critical importance for the discussion and feedback to focus on the 3rd level of skill development. Feedback of the form 'you did quite well I thought' is of little use to promote learning. Feedback of the form 'I noticed his attitude changed as soon as you mentioned the union' or 'I felt really put down when you said "you mean you haven't read Maslow?"', is more likely to promote learning. The Discovery mode of learning requires action and feedback on that action, which of course must be received by the learner. Thus learners receiving feedback will be experiencing the discovery mode of learning, but those giving it will not, at that moment in time. They may be receiving a skill input, or just helping the process along, or have moved into a useful and associated element of cognitive learning. If, however, the learner is rejecting the feedback being offered, learning may not be taking place and the facilitator may need to make some intervention at at a process level.

Example of facilitating behaviour. The
facilitator elicits some feedback to a learner
(Fred) who has just concluded a negotiation, from
the other party (Joan) having just stopped a video
playback.

> "I've stopped the tape there because Joan looked
> very uncomfortable at that point (turns to
> Joan). Joan can you recall how you felt at
> that point and tell us what it was that Fred
> said that made you feel like that?"

REFLECTION

The essence of this mode of learning is that it is
a totally internal process and can occur at any
time. Many designs of experiential learning focus
heavily on discovery but seem to assume that
reflection will occur at some unspecified time,
like at the bar, in the coffee break, in the bath,
or worse still, back at work (when the learner may
be struggling with a week's backlog of work
following a workshop). The fact that it can happen
at any time does not mean that it does. In the
approach described in subsequent chapters,
deliberate action is included in the design to
ensure that it does happen as far as this is
possible. But what exactly is reflection in the
context of skill learning?

This may at first sight be more difficult to
imagine as a mode of learning. In cognitive
learning it includes such processs as assimulation
and accommodation. In the skill area it includes
the following.

1. Valuing - that this new/different way of doing
    things is better than the way I do it now.
2. Choosing - that of the various alternatives
    this is a better way for me.
3. Integrating - one bit of behaviour or skill
    with another.
4. Personalising - i.e. developing an
    individualised way of doing things - this way
    suits me best.
5. Gaining confidence - feeling that I can operate

this way in the future, particularly back on the job. If this last is reported as learning by learners, it represents a high degree of skill development, e.g. 'I now feel confident I can handle a situation like that back at work'.

In the skill area, discovery learning occurs with action and appropriate feedback, learning by reception-of-input results from modelling, but how can reflection learning be accomplished? Reflective learning can take place in isolation, i.e. a retreat, meditation, taking time out to think it through, taking stock of where we are up to, etc.. This is also likely to occur in 'natural' learning on-the-job. In the context of facilitated learning it is most likely that reflective learning will only follow from discovery or reception-of-input learning. It can be facilitated by such activities as leaving space (time) in the programme for it to happen, offering alternative models of behaviour to choose from, comparing results and feedback, getting group consensus on effectiveness of behaviours, allowing people to plan a total interaction which has been practiced in bits and developing their own way of doing things. I have not found any examples of deliberate facilitation of reflective learning in the skill area in any of the literature reviewed.

Some practical situations where reflective learning may occur are.

(a) where a learner has made a presentation to the rest of the group on a presentation skills module, and has received feedback. The presentation is then modelled by two more learners who do it differently and also get feedback. The original learner is then invited to have a think about how she would like to do it differently, taking ideas from the other two modellings;

(b) a learner who has practised a particular type of behaviour and got better and more comfortable with it and gets very positive and supportive feedback. As a result of this he makes a firm commitment with himself to try it out on the very next occasion that presents itself.

68

Reflection can by definition be quite spontaneous and all the facilitator has to do is make sure that it is happening. On the other hand the facilitator may feel that it would be appropriate to stimulate reflection by suitable interventions or the setting of reflective tasks. One simple but effective way of doing this is to ask learners at quite frequent intervals to record what they have learned.

As with the other modes of learning it is important that reflection is at the appropriate level (Level 3). Thus reflecting that 'I feel really good about the way he responded' may be important but needs to proceed to the level of '... as a result of my confronting him about his lateness'.

Example of facilitating behaviour. Facilitator invites learner to personalise some behaviour:

> "Right, we have seen how Mike did that, and then we saw the way Roger did it, then Sue showed us a quite new approach, so will you Harry take 10 minutes out and select the bits from any of the 3 alternative approaches we have seen; add in any ideas you now have, and go through the interview again with Joan, but do it using your words in a way you feel comfortable with."

WHOLE CYCLE LEARNING

Kolb and Fry suggest the desirability of continuous unbroken cycles of learning (Kolb and Fry, 1976). In skill development activities this suggests that all three modes of learning should be linked together in continuous cycles. A diagrammatic representation of such whole cycle learning is shown in Figure 6.3 and is based on an original model due to Burgoyne (sometimes referred to as the Lancaster model) (see Binsted, 1980). It is a model based on a single learner, and the concept of an inner world from which the learner plans and acts in the outer world in which he operates.

As had already been pointed out each mode of learning is different but is necessary for complete or whole learning. What must be remembered, however, is that facilitation of each mode is different.

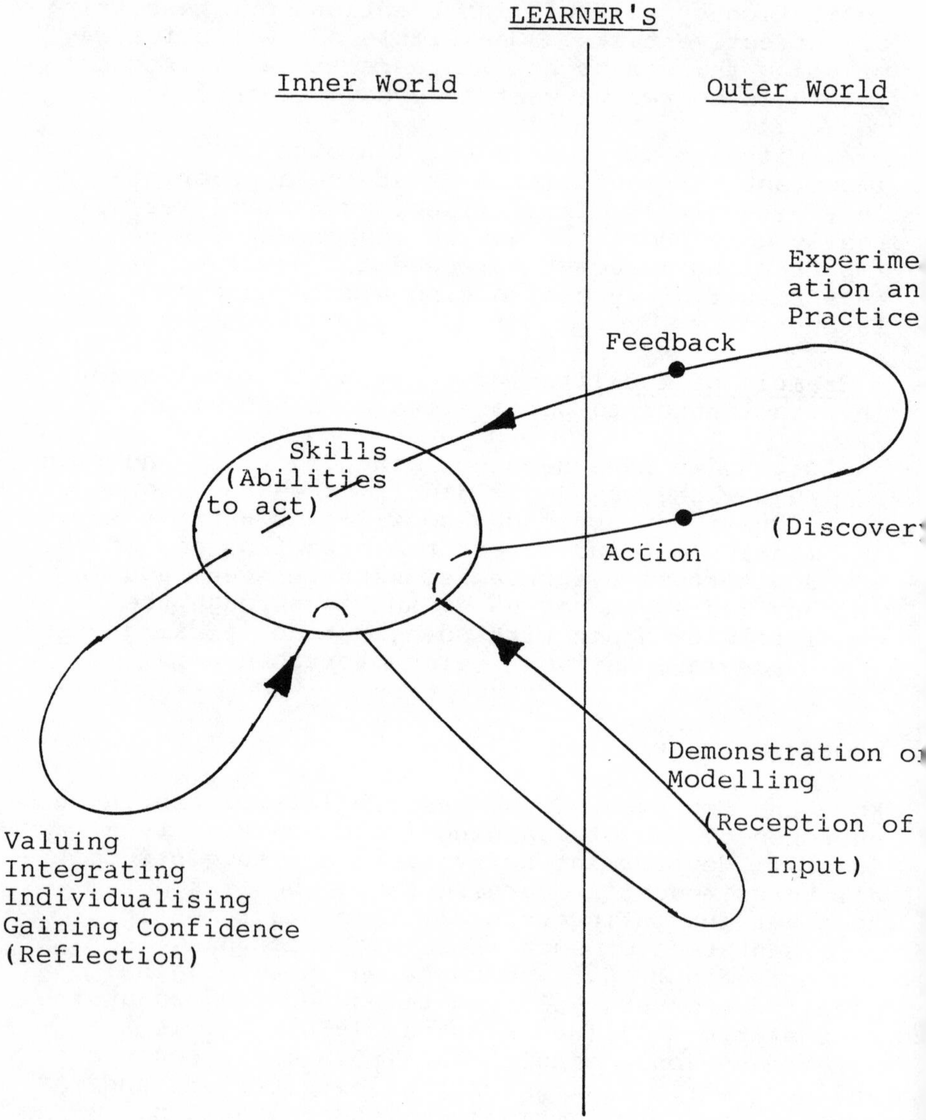
LEARNER'S
Inner World
Outer World
Experime
ation an
Practice
Feedback
Skills
(Abilities
to act)
(Discover
Action
Demonstration o
Modelling
(Reception of
Input)
Valuing
Integrating
Individualising
Gaining Confidence
(Reflection)

Figure 6.4

Thus a strategy for developing skills is likely to be most effective if it includes all the modes of learning, in linked continuous cycles. I term this 'whole cycle learning'. From the designers point of view this strategy can then be implemented in many ways using any suitable vehicles. This concept of 'whole cycle learning' provides a further conceptual framework for understanding skill development activities. The more traditional methods of using role plays, exercises, games, structured experiences, etc., rely solely on a discovery learning cycle, which may be a one off or repeated activity. The more recent developments (which would appear to work more effectively) link modelling with practice and feedback (reception of input followed by discovery), and are described by Shaw, Tosti, Israel and Jones, Wellins and Guinn (Shaw 1981, Tosti 1980, Israel 1977, Jones 1980, and Wellins and Guinn, 1985).

The next chapter suggests how these ideas can be developed into practical designs.

SUMMARY

Three modes of learning can be involved in skill development activities modelling, discovery and valuing/personalising. The examples given illustrate each mode of learning and give a typical fragment of facilitating behaviour. The idea of 'whole cycle' learning is introduced in which all three modes are linked together. This gives a basis for designing learning activities.

7 Strategies for design and vehicles for learning

<u>Choosing the elements of the learning cycle and the order to put them in. Choosing the learning method and media, and the vehicles for learning</u>.

DESIGN STRATEGIES

Having established some principles for effective skill development such as the need for skill definitions at Level 3, raising awareness, the need to develop the ability to act, and whole cycle learning, there is now a need to explore how such principles can be integrated into a design strategy.

To design a learning activity for interpersonal skill development, a number of choices have to be made. They relate to 3 aspects of design.

1. The order in which the various elements of the learning cycle should occur, which define the total learning <u>process</u>.

2. The learning __method__ to be involved (including media).
3. The __vehicles__ to be provided.

THE ORDER OF THE LEARNING CYCLES

Whole cycles of learning can be built from the 3 modes in any order. An example is: a demonstration of how to conduct a selection interview, on video (reception of input) followed by practice with feedback in a trio of learners, which is videoed (discovery) followed by consideration and private counselling with a facilitator using the video, about how to behave in the future (reflection).

   Another example, using the cycles in a different order would be where a small group of learners experiment with an opening for a sales interaction (with one member taking the role of the customer) which is evaluated by the group (discovery) followed by thinking about how to do it differently (reflection) followed by another member of the group, or the facilitator modelling an alternative approach (reception of input for the rest of the group).

   As has already been pointed out, different people in the learner group may be engaged in different parts of the cycle of learning at any one time, but it can be arranged that each learner is involved in whole cycles over a period of a total learning event; but more of this later.

   On the assumption that a design for a learning activity is going to involve several cycles of whole cycle learning, it can be argued that it does not much matter where we start, since all three modes will be used several times over. Although not disagreeing with this, there is another dimension to this choice which can be demonstrated from the two examples just cited. This dimension relates to the tutor learner relationship and the general 'feel' of the activity. In the first example of the video demonstration, a somewhat learner dependant situation is signalled. The video demonstration is a 'this is the way to do it' model, and the feedback and counselling may then

lean towards giving feedback about how well the
learner did compared with the model. Much will
depend on the facilitating behaviour of the
facilitator, but the design may pre-empt this. In
the second example the group is in an experimental
situation, literally trying to discover what works
best. This suggests either an interdependant or
independant learner relationship with the
facilitator (Binsted and Snell, 1981). In such a
design the tutor may join the group or may only be
concerned with guiding the process. However this
is not the whole story, because the methods used
also effect the situation.

THE LEARNING METHOD

Choice of learning method will also influence the
learning process as experienced by the learner.
Using the example of conducting a selection
interview just given (reception of input,
discovery, reflection), the methods described are:

(a) the demonstration model on video,
(b) the practice carried out in trios, one person
    interviewing another, with the third as
    observer. The observer and the interviewee
    would give feedback reinforcing correct
    behaviour and refer back to the video;
(c) interviewer only reviews the video and engagesin
    a private counselling session, which helps the
    learner to personalise his experience, and
    reinforces good behaviour to increase
    self-esteem and confidence.

   At first sight this combination of mode sequence
and method could produce a dependant learner
relationship and could be seen as heavily oriented
to a conditioning philosophy of learning. A quite
different philosophy could be enacted using the
same order of reception of input, discovery and
reflection, but using different methods. For
example:

(a) the input could be achieved by asking a member
     of the group to show the rest of the group how
     he conducts such an interview. This could
     then be discussed and certain key skills
     identified;

74

(b)   the discovery phase could be set up in trios as
       before, but feedback would be non-evaluative,
       and concentrate on how the interviewer and the
       person being interviewed <u>felt</u> at various
       points, and how this interview compared with
       the first;
(c)   the reflective phase could involve people
       considering and selecting behaviours they have
       seen others use, and trying these out for
       themselves, or deciding how they would do it
       next time. Such a design would be enacting an
       experiential philosophy of learning.

    Thus both the choice of method and the sequence
of cycles are together going to influence the
'feel' and therefore the outcome of a learning
event.

THE VEHICLE

What now remains is to design or select an
appropriate vehicle for the learning. The vehicle
provides among other things the content that is
implicit in most interpersonal interactions. For
example if working with a group of pharmaceutical
representatives, on their interaction with a general
medical practitioner, the vehicle could be a case
study which would contain details of the product to
be presented, a description of the G.P. and the
previous relationship with the representative etc..
This could form the basis of a role play. This case
study would need to contain technical, commercial
and personal data and would act as a vehicle for
learning to take place.

    Vehicles can be classified into:

1.   work experience (i.e. work situations that the
      learner has actually experienced in carrying
      out a work role);
2.   projects;
3.   interactive case studies;
4.   games;
5.   simulation;
6.   structured experiences;
7.   instant case studies.

	WORK EXPERIENCE	PROJECTS OR ASSIGNMENTS	INTERACTIVE CASE STUDIES	GAMES	SIMULATIONS & ROLE PLAYS	STRUCTURED EXPERIENCES	INSTANT INTERACTIVE CASE STUDIES
BASIS	Work situation with learner in job role	Work situation with learner not in job role	Contrived to facilitate specific learning				Learning event based (what goes on in the learner group) Work role based
LEARNER BEHAVIOUR	Real time action		Reacting to historical account	Rule governed	Role governed	Free experimentation	
EXAMPLES	Debrief on a live encounter by the learner. Working through real problems with a group in team development workshop.	Assignments inside organisation to get learner into action followed by debriefing in coaching	"Real life" past happenings (often not learner's "real life") to feed into group work e.g. role play	Inter group interactions, etc. followed by group work/debriefing	Role plays. Interactions set up to focus on particular skills or issues. Task which involves I.P. skills	Tasks + 'here and now' activities Exercises from "collections"	Replays of work situations. Learner being himself
WHAT HAS TO BE PROVIDED/AVAILABLE	Access for tutor to observe	Remit, problem definition	Details written up, or film video, etc.	Method of scoring, rules, constraints, briefs	Definition of task and content, process of interactions and/or roles, briefs	Tasks and exercises, briefing sheets, instruments	Generally nothing except learner experience

Figure 7.1 Vehicles for interpersonal skill development

These can be conveniently differentiated in the
model in Figure 7.1.

1. Work Experience

This is where an actual work experience, with the
learner in a job role, is used as a vehicle for
learning. The most obvious example is a coaching
situation with a boss being present when a
subordinate is dealing, for example, with a
disciplinary matter. After the interview the boss
does an unscheduled coaching session. This form of
'curb-stone coaching' is popular in sales training
(Cover, 1980). Another quite different example is
the sort of activity which might be included as
part of a team development programme, when the team
are doing a routine task, using real time work
experience on site, as a way of focusing on and
developing their interpersonal skills.

   Work experience provides a very high reality
learning situation. It requires that the tutor not
only has access to the situation, but can take a
role which does not interfere with the interaction.
For example, in sales training the boss will make a
call with the salesman, but must take minimal part
in the interaction, and certainly restrain himself
from taking over the interview. This may be quite
different to achieve if the customer keeps steering
the conversation in his direction, thinking that
there must be some advantage in talking to the
boss. Alternatively, if the facilitator can get a
group to bring its work and environment away with
it, then off site development may have advantages
as far as the internal workings of the group are
concerned. Specific approaches to the informal
coaching are given in Chapters 11 and 12.

2. Projects or Assignments

These are real life situations which are used for
development purposes although the learner is not in
a job or other permanent role. The use of projects
is common in Business Schools and long courses,
whereas the use of assignments are more likely to
be found inside organisations. They are not
generally used for interpersonal skill development,

although there seems no reason why they should not be. As with 'work experience', suitable de-briefing or coaching would be required, to ensure whole cycle learning.

3. Interactive Case Studies

These are based on real life situations which are transferred into the learning situation as a vehicle for learning. The traditional way of doing this is with text. These case studies have to be read and in the interpersonal skill development field, often take the form of briefings for role plays, or inter group activities. The fact that they are based on real life situations may be of little advantage in the interpersonal skills area especially if the learners do not share a similar reality. In-company examples would be much more likely to conform to this requirement, since the learner group would share the same reality. Due to the difficulty of adequately describing skills, behaviours and situations, text based case studies must always be inferior to filmed or video based material.

In any event the case study can be used to initiate group work, and is particularly useful when learners have no experience of the interactions for which they are developing their skills. Approaches which start with a definitive model of the 'right way to do it' fall into this category. The model then forms the basis of rehearsal and feedback.

4. Games

Although the use of games is a large field of education and training research and development, and there are a wide variety of application, some are suitable for interpersonal skill development. In some games the situation may be very unreal, based on a number of rules which govern behaviour. For example, a game which has rules that tend to force groups into win/lose conflict so that certain behaviour can be examined. If feedback is limited to the interactions when the game is in progress, it is difficult to see how whole cycle learning can be achieved. If games are used to

initiate small group work, then whole cycle
learning is feasible. Games are good at generating
inter group behaviours, but again to achieve whole
cycle learning add on activities may often be
required. The rules implicit in a game may force
people into uncharacteristic behaviours but this
may be a useful way of helping people out of their
set patterns of behaviour.

5. Simulations

These can be distinguished from case studies in that
they are not real life situations but simulations
which reflect typical aspects of real life
situations. They differ from games in that they are
not rule governed, though they generally involve
learners playing roles. They can be designed to
focus on desired areas of learning and this may
involve excluding other factors which might inhibit
learning. A good example is the famous Lego tower
exercise which uses a low reality task to focus on
process issues and interpersonal behaviour. Many of
the standard role play exercises fall into this
category. They are most often initiated by some
form of briefing which in some cases is open ended,
and fairly non specific as far as learner behaviour
is concerned. At the other extreme the briefing may
contain detailed instructions for behaviour
approaching an acting script. This is a much used
vehicle in interpersonal skill development
activities and success depends on how well the
learner can identify with the roles (s)he is given.
In my experience there does seem to be a tendency to
over complicate designs to make them 'rich' learning
experiences. This often raises far too many issues
to deal with at the feedback stage, or makes the
task so difficult that failure is almost inevitable.
This can cause feelings of frustration or of being
'set up' by the facilitator and neither outcome is
conducive to learning (Binsted and Snell, 1982).

6. Structured Experiences

These are again very commonly found in
interpersonal skill development activities. They
differ from simulations and role plays in that the

interactions which take place in the learning
situation are too constrained by specifying rules or
roles. Tasks are defined and sometimes processes,
but people are encouraged to be themselves, and not
play a role. Pfeiffer and Jones are a ready source
of examples and ideas for designs of structured
experiences (Pfeiffer and Jones, 1975). Learners
are free to experiment with new behaviours or get
feedback on their own usual styles and
characteristics. The action is kept in the 'here
and now' which means that action and feedback are
focused on what happened in the room rather than
what happens 'back home' on the job. In the
Pfeiffer and Jones collection very precise detail is
given about the learning process and the options
open to the tutor. All types of interaction can be
generated, one to one, one to group, or inter group.
They can be used with experienced or non-experienced
learners, strangers or family groups in the context
of team building. Sometimes structured experiences
are instrumented, i.e. feedback is given using
rating scales, etc..

   In general the role of the facilitator is
critical for success.

Instant Interactive Case Studies

These are always a very fruitful basis for
learning. They fit in somewhere between 'structured
experiences' and 'work experience' on the model
which makes it difficult to place on Figure 7.1.
Instant interactive case studies are generated
within a few minutes from learner experience. They
start as verbal descriptions of a familiar
situation and the interaction involved, with as
much detail as necessary to start a live replay of
the interaction. The replay is the meat of the
instant interactive case study.

   First it is highly relevant and 'real' for the
learner who will have intimate knowledge of the
technical content of the interaction, the context
in which it takes plae and the sort of people who
may be involved. Learner groups from the same
functions within the same organisation will share
enormous quantities of data and common experience.
Even more to the point, I have found it very simple

to get such groups to develop 'instant case studies' in very short spaces of time. The advantage of using work experience can be enhanced by asking the learners to raise the issues or problems that most concern them, thus enabling learning to be around their agenda. This avoids the problem of the facilitator 'scratching them where they don't itch', i.e. working on problems which they do not own. This vehicle can be used with stranger groups, but may not work quite so well. It cannot be used where learners have no relevant experience, e.g. for initial training of new entrants. An 'instant interactive case study' can be set up by a facilitator during a session by merely asking a learner to describe a situation to the point where the total group can identify with it.

THE DESIGN STRATEGY

In this Chapter I have suggested that there are three elements to a design strategy. Each element represents a choice. The three elements involve decisions about which order to sequence the modes of learning, which method or media to use, and which vehicle to use. This presents the facilitator with a complex matrix of options. In a large volume it would be possible to examine them all, and with a large investment of research to do comparative evaluations. This monograph does not attempt to do this, but rather to describe some new approaches which utilise the principles already enunciated, and which have been tried and work rather well in practice. You will no doubt find that many of the ideas and principles can be utilised in contexts other than those described. For example, the small group processes to be described can be initiated using any of the vehicles just defined. However, they will all have different effects on the learner group depending on the composition of the group. For example, a mature in-company group will probably react best to an instant case study vehicle, whereas a group with no work experience would not be able to do that. They might respond best to a simple non-threatening structured experience.

SUMMARY

Starting from the principle of whole cycle learning
there are three elements suggested for a design
strategy, upon which design decisions have to be
made.

1. The sequence of the three different modes of
   learning.
2. The learning method used (including the
   media).
3. The vehicle to generate appropriate
   interactions for learning to take place.

Only some of the possibilities will be examined in
subsequent Chapters.

8 Setting up and running small group work (the episodic approach)

> One of two approaches in which whole cycle learning can be achieved by dealing with an interaction, episode by episode.

As discussed in the previous chapter, there are many variations which can be used in different circumstances, to achieve interpersonal skill development. This faces the facilitator with a number of choices involving the cycles of learning, the method and media and the vehicles for learning. The approach which follows utilise all the principles already presented and is suitable for off the job training activities, courses, workshops or learning sets.

   The implication is that a facilitator is present, although the approach can also be effective in self development groups. The approach involves some structuring of activities and always involves a group of learners, the minimum size of which will become apparent.

THE TRADITIONAL APPROACH

The most common structure to be found in traditional approaches to group work is the three part 'brief task debrief' sequence (Binsted and Snell, 1982). The facilitator role is most commonly:

1. to give the brief for the task as a set of instructions and check for understanding;
2. to observe the interaction during the task, making notes, or indexing a video recording, without getting directly involved with doing the task,
3. to guide a de-brief session which includes such activities as giving and eliciting feedback from the group, recalling specific episodes, reporting results, giving inputs or developing discussion (Binsted and Snell, 1982). All this would be based on the interactions which took place during the task.

This structure is often too rigid for the effective development of interpersonal skills, and does not in general develop the ability to act. It is quite adequate for cognitive learning to take place, or for raising awareness. This structure also relies heavily on a single discovery learning cycle.

The vehicles most used are games, simulations and structured experiences (as defined in Chapter 7). What follows is a description of an approach which incorporates the principles of whole cycle learning and results in developing specifically defined interpersonal skills.

DEALING WITH AN INTERACTION EPISODE AT A TIME (THE EPISODIC APPROACH)

In this approach the interaction is started and then stopped to learn from each episode, rather than taking the whole interaction at once. Each episode of the interaction which may only last a few minutes, then becomes the basis for a whole cycle learning activity with several cycles of discovery, modelling and reflection. An example will illustrate this. A group is composed of six managers who are working on the problem of how to discuss below standard performance with a subordinate who refuses to acknowledge it. This is set in the context of their companies' formal staff appraisal system. The managers produce an instant interactive case study based on their past experience of such situations. They thus supply all the content of the interaction. The learning process follows the steps now described.

1. Setting up

The facilitator identifies the person who will start the process off. Some member of the group who has high ownership of the problem would be most suitable. The skill to be worked on is discussed and defined at all three levels as far as this is possible (as discussed in Chapter 3). This includes the 'situation of action' (e.g. is the interaction an informal chat in the office or part of a formal appraisal interview). The definition will include 'effective behaviour' such as 'dealing with rejection of the manager's data but minimising the reduction of the subordinates self-esteem'. Whether or not the 'dimensions of ability' are defined at this stage will depend on a number of factors (e.g. if they were actually known, if the facilitator wishes to 'teach' a particular way of dealing with the problem, or if the group wishes to experiment with a range of possibilities).

The learner selected to start the process off (who we will call the 'initiator') may then need some time to think out what he wants to do, e.g. what aspect of performance he wants to raise and how he is going to cope with the subordinate's rejection of his criticism. It will also be necessary to identify a manager who will take the part of the subordinate, who may also need a short preparation time.

2. Getting into action

The facilitator now sets up the interaction as shown in Figure 8.1. He lets the interaction run for a short time only, generally for one episode. In this context an episode is that part of an interaction which has a clearly defined beginning and an end. When a new episode begins, the pattern

of behaviour generally changes. In this example
behaviour is aimed at 'putting the person at ease'
might form the first episode of the interview.

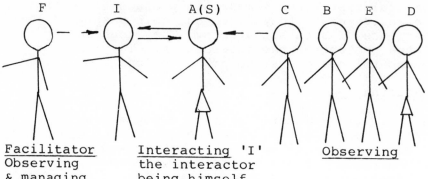

Figure 8.1 Setting up the Interaction

3. Generating feedback

The facilitator stops the process at the end of an
episode, and generates feedback from the group
being careful to tap the various sources of data in
order to minimise contamination, e.g. asking the
'subordinate' how she felt rather than first asking
the observers if they thought she looked nervous.
This principle of minimising contamination is most
important, since it ensures the highest quality of
feedback data the group is capable of generating.
One important skill in interacting with others is
the ability to 'read' the other person's feelings
and emotional state. Eliciting data in the order
described gives feedback to the observers on this
dimension (and the initiator).

   If for example the subordinate did reveal that
she felt apprehensive this might be powerful
feedback to an observer who did not notice this and
is surprised by her comment.

Facilitating feedback is discussed in Chapter 14.
The group interaction is shown diagrammatically
in Figure 8.2

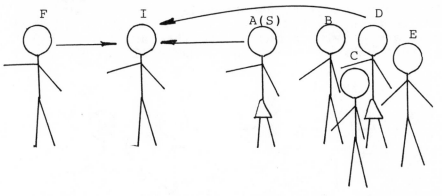

Facilitator	Initiator	Subordinate	Observers
stops process. Gives and/or elicits feedback	receiving feedback	giving feed- back	giving feedback

Figure 8.2 Generating Feedback

The learning process might be quite complex
because different people will be going through
different parts of the cycle at any one instant.
It can be anticipated, however, that the initiator
'I' is going through the feedback part of a
discovery cycle, 'A' is getting and exploring her
behavioural feedback (see Chapter 14) by being on
the receiving end of an interview which she
normally gives (discovery and reflection), the
observers are watching the modelling of one form of
behaviour, thus getting a skill input.

4. Modelling Alternative Behaviour

The facilitator then asks the group to suggest
alternative behaviour. Facilitating behaviour
could be.

"Can anyone think of another way of doing it?"
of "How would you do it Jack?", or focusing
more accurately on the 'dimensions of ability'

"What could 'I' have done to make 'A' more at ease and less hostile?"

As soon as suggestions are made the person who makes them is invited to show the group what (s)he means, and model one end of the interaction, in a different way, as shown diagrammatically in Figure 8.3.

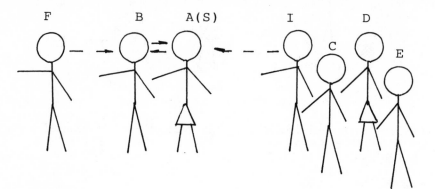

Setting up	Interacting	Observing
alternative	'B' taking	including 'I'
behaviour	interview	
	as manager.	
	'A' reacting	
	as subordinate	

Figure 8.3 Modelling Alternative Behaviour

It can be anticipated that 'B' is now going through the action part of a discovery cycle, 'I' is receiving a skill input from modelling by 'B'.

The facilitator then repeats steps 3 and 4 for as many times as necessary to generate alternative new behaviours.

5. Trying it Out

The tutor then asks 'I' to think about what he has seen and go through the episode again the way he now feels he could do it best. He is also invited to continue with the interaction past the first episode, and onto the second. The process is now similar to the getting into action step shown in Figure 8.1. It can be anticipated that 'I' has reflected and personalised the modelling he has seen and then begins another discovery cycle. The facilitator then repeats steps 3-5 for as many times as is required for the second episode, not forgetting to generate feedback the first time round on episode one and two.

General Points

This process continues episode by episode through the whole interaction, using different members of the group and keeping the whole group as involved and active as possible. The size of the group may be quite small and can work with a minimum of two people, who have to reverse roles each time. This gives a very limited opportunity for modelling alternative behaviour. A bigger group results in more variety and ideas, but 10-12 is getting rather big.

Summary of Process (Episodic)

1. Set up group.   Repeat
2. Get interaction started.
3. Stop at end of episode and generate feedback
4. Get someone to model alternative behaviour.
5. Invite initiator to try it again and then
   continue with next episode.

VARIATIONS

It must be emphasised that the example just given is only one example of the episodic approach to using the learning principles already enunciated. This example is one of the most informal versions of the approach and utilises instant interactive case studies (see Chapter 7).

More formality can be introduced in the setting up Step 1. For example, prepared case studies may be used in which the interactions and the background are all described in detail. The same can be done with games or simulations or structured

experiences. All are means of getting an
interaction going. It must be stated, however,
that case studies must be designed for skill
development and not for cognitive learning alone.
The most obvious category of activity to get the
interaction going is what is generally referred to
as role plays. These may be simulations or case
studies. All can be linked to the approach just
described although it should be recognised that in
the example given every effort was made to avoid
role playing. This can be done by asking people to
act out situations in which they are themselves, or
in their job role (i.e. generating instant
interactive case studies). In the example given
only 'A' would be in danger of playing a role, and
this could be diminished by asking 'I' to interview
'A' on an aspect of her real life performance in
her job role. The difficulty associated with role
plays will be discussed more fully in Chapter 17.

It also helps if the facilitator asks people 'to
be the salesman' or 'take the role of the salesman'
(rather than play it).

Video recordings of the interaction can be added
to the example just given, but restricted to
recording 'I's' interaction only. Playback can be
given in the style of a counselling session with
facilitator and learner alone. The effect of this
is generally very positive since the learner 'I' is
looking at his first attempt to carry out the
interaction followed immediately (on the tape) by
his re-play which is drawing on modelling from the
rest of the group. He thus sees himself improve.

The essence of this approach is to work on each
episode of behaviour in an interaction in such a
way that a learner experiences whole cycle learning
for each episode. This in practice means that the
facilitator needs to stop the interaction at the
end of the episode. This requires some particular
skills on his part.

FACILITATING SKILLS

The main problem is when to stop. If the
interaction goes on too long, and in some instances

10 minutes can be too long, it becomes more and more difficult to remember what happened in the early stages. The amount of data to share can become excessive, and several different episodes may be involved, all of which require re-modelling. The easiest way to recognise the end of an episode is when the end has just been passed. This is generally marked by a behaviour change. For example, in a selection interview the first episode may be a quite short 'hello, hope you had a good journey, sit down' ritual. It may be followed by a 'I see from your application form ...' questioning sequence. In such a situation the end of the first episode is clearly signalled by the first sentence in the second.

Another factor is to look out for the likelihood of important data being generated which should not be lost. This can be a reason for stopping part way through a long episode. One way of doing that would be for the facilitator to say something like 'Joan has been looking very uncomfortable for the last few minutes, I wonder if we could stop and find out what she is feeling?'

The learners may on occasions express some frustration with stopping the process and may need some explanation of the rationale behind the approach. This raises the question of whether it would not be a good idea to explain the rationale and the process before the session started. In general I am personally in favour of doing this as a matter of principle. However, my experience with this approach has been that the more I explain, the more difficult it is to start. My mode of operation now is to say nothing and go straight into the setting up step, and pick up any questions about the method if they arise, which they generally do not. There are, however, occasions when this episodic approach is not the best, when for example stopping the interaction may actually destroy it, or if the total interaction is one long episode. In this event the approach described in the next Chapter will be the one to use. It is very difficult to generalise any conditions when this is the case, but experience with both this approach and the one described in the next Chapter will clarify this point.

SUMMARY

In this Chapter one approach to setting up and
running learning activities in small groups is
described. Some degree of structure is involved
and the context is a workshop or a course. In this
Chapter the approach involves dealing with the
interaction episode by episode and creating a whole
cycle learning for each episode.

9 Setting up and running small group work (the stored approach)

The second approach in which whole cycle learning can be achieved, when breaking the interaction down into episodes would be dysfunctional.

THE STORED APPROACH

This alternative approach is again for developing interpersonal skills in small groups in the contexts of a workshop or course. This approach may be useful when the interruptions described in the episodic approach would be dysfunctional. This approach must employ video recording of the total interaction. The group then work off the recording which has stored the interaction.

1. Setting up

The setting up step is identical with the episodic approach and can work off case studies, simulations, structured exercises, or instant interactive case studies.

2. Recording the interaction

The facilitator video records the entire interaction, indexing as she goes along and noting key episodes, behaviour, or particular abilities (or lack of them). It can be useful to give the observers assigned tasks to look out for specified aspects of the interaction. The process is as in Figure 8.1, but with the facilitator video recording the total interaction between 'I' and 'A', e.g. a whole appraisal interview.

3. Reflection

At this point it is good to get the group to reflect on what they have seen and learned so far. This is conveniently done by asking them to write it down for sharing later.

4. Generating feedback (from video)

The facilitator now plays back an episode from the video tape, and generates feelings and feedback about the episode shown.

Typical facilitating behaviour can be, e.g. 'What did you feel like when he said that, think yourself back to that point in the interview'. Again the need to focus on the 'dimensions of ability' should be emphasised. Such questions as 'What was it that "I" said that made "A" feel like she did?' achieve this.

The process here is similar to that shown in Figure 8.2, but from the video. Additionally the direct feedback from the video is also present and can be very powerful by itself particularly in a negative sense of showing low ability (which is why it is so important to move on from that point). The learning process is similar to Step 3 of the episodic approach. This way of developing feedback and reliving past events from videotape is similar to the principles of Interpersonal Process Recall (IPR) (Kagan, 1982). Ideas from that approach are very relevant, particularly the principle of letting the learner control the video replay, via a remote control device, and the 'Inquirer' role of the facilitator. As reported by Klein and Smith,

involvement of the rest of the group is also
essential, but I have not found it necessary to
impose the sort of rules which they found
beneficial (Klein and Smith, 1981). The group
become quickly accustomed to the process.

5. Modelling alternative behaviour

The facilitator then asks the group to suggest
alternative behaviour and then asks them to
demonstrate what they mean. The process is the same
as that shown in Figure 8.3, with different people
moving in to take different parts.

6. Generating feedback (live)

After a learner has modelled some alternative
behaviour, the facilitator again generates feedback
in exactly the same ways as shown in Figure 8.2.

The facilitator will repeat steps 5 and 6 as
necessary.

7. Trying it out

The facilitator then asks 'I' to think about what
he has seen and to have another go at the same
episode. The learning process is the same as for
step 5 of the episodic approach.

   The facilitator repeats steps 4-7 gradually
progressing through the tape.

Summary of process (stored)   Repeat

1. ┌Set up group.
2. ├Get interaction started and video record.
3. ├Group reflects.
4. ├Replay part of video and generate feedback.
5.┌├Get someone to model alternative behaviour.
6.├└Generate feedback (live). ──────────────────►
7.└──Invite initiator to try episode again.──────►

   One choice in this approach is that only some of
the more interesting episodes are worked through
and particularly the ones that the initiator is
most concerned about. However, in practice it is
more difficult to get the modelling of alternative

behaviour going. I suspect this is because the process of video replay is more familiar in the context of traditional approaches and sessions may tend to regress to those more familiar, but less effective traditional methods.

VARIATIONS

The most fundamental variation of the 'stored' approach is to start with a pre-filmed/recorded interaction involving people other than the group. Although in the past there have been some popular management films which seem to specialise in showing how not to do things, there are now approaches being used which start with modelling the right way to handle an interaction. In its simplest form this involves showing the learners the film or video and then getting them to copy and practice the required behaviour. This generally enacts a conditioning approach to learning and relies on reinforcing correct behaviour. Examples of this variation are given by a number of authors.

Israel describes the use of 'the perfect sales model' which trainees practise (called behavioural rehearsals) and are then given positive reinforcement. They are encouraged to focus on 'dimensions of ability' via feedback forms. This approach is used in the context of retail selling (Israel 1977).

Jones describes video taped models of behaviour using experienced people, demonstrating the 'right' way to act. He provides a comprehensive basis of theory and links the approach to both respondent and operant conditioning and observational learning (Jones, 1981).

Daniels refers to the sociological concept that 'behavioural modelling is the fundamental method which conditions humans to assume normative behaviour in their own culture', and then goes to on to explain the pitfalls to be avoided in making a 'master performer' model (Daniels, 1981).

Tosti emphasised the need to avoid poor quality 'master performances' and lists some reasons for poor quality. He goes on to point out reasons why practice and feedback sessions alone are ineffective (Tosti, 1980).

All these approaches are referred to as 'behavioural modelling' and are based on conditioning theories of learning. For the more sophisticated skills of management these approaches are less suitable. The use of modelling in the approaches described in this monograph is more creative and is used for exploring 'dimensions of ability', experimenting with alternative behaviours, etc.. Modelling used in this way can form part of the enactment of any of the learning theories (but see Chapter 14).

Another variation described by Wellins and Guinn is based on the practice that the facilitator models correct behaviour, which has the effect of producing learner dependence. They propose ways of countering this, which will be discussed in Chapter 16 (Wellins and Guinn, 1985).

Another approach developed by the University of London Teaching Methods Unit is to get groups to look at videotaped vignettes and then ask them to discuss what they would do next. This aproach is based on a dramatised case study and contains no modelling or practice. However, the idea of starting the process off with a dramatised case study is useful when the group has no experience to draw on, and could be followed by getting the group to continue acting out the interaction which would allow either the 'episodic' or the 'stored' approaches already described to be proceeded with, thus allowing whole cycle learning.

COMPARISONS

Comparing the two approaches described in this and the previous Chapter with those more usually found (based on the brief-task-debrief design) using interactive case studies, simulations, structured experiences, etc., there are a number of significant differences summarised in Table 9.1.

97

Table 9.1

Commonly used approaches using case studies, simulations, etc.	Approaches described in this monograph using instant case studies
1. Based on tasks or situations devised or recorded by facilitator.	Uses experience of the learners who provide their own content, background, etc.
2. Single cycle of learning, generally. Brief, task, feed-back/debrief. Often limited to discovery only.	Whole cycle learning. Interaction, feedback, generation of alter-native behaviour, modelling, reflection, choice.
3. Feedback normally restricted to verbal.	Alternative behaviour modelled and worked on.
4. Feedback can be pre-dominantly negative pointing out faults and what the learner ought to have done.	Feedback supplemented by demonstrating alternative behaviour for learner to choose from.
5. Often limited involve-ment of learners in feedback process.	Highly active role in feedback and modelling alternative behaviour
6. Balance of learning tends to be cognitive.	Balance of learning is skill development with cognitive and affective as well.

1. In the approach described using the instant interactive case study maximum use is made of learners' experience in the area in which learning is to take place. They generate the background and content of the interactions. The interactions thus have high reality and relieve the facilitator of the need to generate content (indeed he need not even understand it, if it is highly technical). This tends to generate high interest in the session, high motivation to learn and increase the possibility of transfer back on the job.

2. The design based on modelling follows the pattern (repeated several times over).

   Interaction
   Feedback
   Generation of alternative behaviour
   Reflection and choice
   Trying out new behaviour.

   The design is multi-cycle and produces whole cycle learning. The more usually found design is in the form.

   Brief
   Activity (task/case study, etc.)
   Feedback and debrief

   in one single cycle. This generally only utilises discovery learning with no modelling or reflection built in. However, other types of learning may be present resulting from such things as verbal input from the trainer in the debrief about some aspect of the interaction or behaviour. This is more likely to result in cognitive learning as distinct from skill development (Binsted and Snell, 1982).

3. Verbal feedback clearly has its uses and may form a first step in a feedback process. It is most effective for facilitating cognitive learning from an experiential activity or for raising awareness of skills. It is not, however, adequate for developing 'abilities to act'. The reason for this is that it is quite easy to describe 'situations of action' and

'effective behaviour' but often very difficult to describe 'dimensions of ability' which is the level at which the learning needs to take place. You will no doubt notice that I have tended to demonstrate some of the 'dimensions of ability' that facilitators might use, rather than attempt to describe them (by offering forms of words). In this approach descriptive feedback is minimised and alternative behaviour is acted out. This moving out of verbal descriptive feedback into alternative active behaviour is a key facilitator not generally found in the more traditional approaches which often rely entirely on verbal feedback.

4. Feedback can be predominantly negative and take the form of (constructive?) criticism, pointing out mistakes or errors. I have spoken to trainers who clearly believe that pointing out errors is an essential ingredient for facilitating learning. The way it is sometimes expressed is 'what can be done in a role play when someone does it really well first time?'. At best, in some designs, the learner gets an idea of what they ought to do but have little idea of how to improve their ability to act. For example, a learner may be told 'to be more friendly, warmer', at the beginning of an interview. But that is what he thought he was being. Without demonstrating alternative behaviour (which gets down to dimensions of ability) learners can get locked into their own incompetence.

5. Another feature of the more commonly used approaches to skill development is that feedback sessions are often facilitator dominated and untapped but valuable data, feelings etc., reside in the learners. In some of the sessions which have been researched, the feedback developed into a 'talk on' by the facilitator. In the approaches described in this monograph, picking up data, feelings and ideas for alternative behaviour from learners is another fundamental aspect of the approach. Apart from keeping everybody highly involved there are two other advantages.

(i)   learners put their ideas 'on the line' when
      they model behaviour and get feedback on
      how well these work out in practice;
(ii) the richness of the session is greatly
      increased.

6. The research already referred to (Binsted and
    Snell, 1982) indicated a heavy bias towards
    cognitive learning in the more traditional
    approaches. This could be due to a quite
    legitimate desire for that sort of learning to
    be the outcome. If more balanced learning is
    required including skill development, then both
    from a theoretical point of view and as a
    result of field trials, it appears that the
    principles and approaches here described do
    work.

CONCLUSIONS

The key to the approaches described is the
inclusion of modelling of behaviour. Learners are
encouraged to behave in the way they think is most
appropriate in the situation. Such behaviour is
thus complex in that it will involve both verbal
and non-verbal elements and will stem from
concepts, feelings, values and beliefs. It should
not be assumed that the approach focuses only on
the verbal element of the interaction which could
result in seeking only a form of words or verbal
patterning. The balance between the elements of
the interaction can be adjusted by the type of
feedback generated within the learner group. This
could vary from a discussion of beliefs and the
congruence of certain behaviour, on the one hand to
searching for a form of words 'How can you say that
so as not to give offence?' on the other.

In all the examples given, the assumption has
been that skill being developed involves learners
interacting with other people, e.g. managers with
subordinates, salespeople with customers, etc.

The example shown in the Figures 8.1 to 8.3
involve one to one interactions. The approaches
are just as suitable for one to group interactions.
The only difference is that the size for the group

that the learner can interact with is the size of
the learner group less one. At the first phase of
the process the corresponding diagram to Figure 8.1
is Figure 9.1 below.

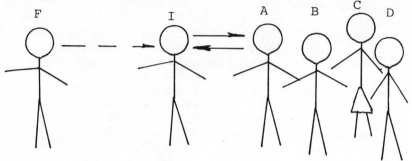

Facilitator   Interaction
observing and   'I' interacting
facilitating   with rest of group
process.   who are being, say, a
                             subordinate team.

Figure 9.1 One to Group Interactions

   The principles are also valid if the skills being
developed are those involved in a group interacting
with itself (as in a team development event).
Although I have not done extensive field trials my
experience of team building supports my contention
that modelling alternative behaviour is very
effective in this context.

SUMMARY

The 'stored' approach is described where it would be
dysfunctional to stop the initial interaction being
learned about. Both the stored and the episodic
approach are compared with the more traditional
approaches. One key element missing in those
latter is any modelling of alternative behaviour.

10 Self development activities covering chapters 5–9

These activities are designed to help you explore your current design strategies (or the design strategies embedded in the activities you run) to practice giving and eliciting feedback, developing 'instant interactive case studies', and try out the 'episodic' and 'stored' approaches.

MENU OF ACTIVITIES

Activity 6: this involves analysing a skill development activity in terms of a development strategy, suggesting alternatives and testing these out.

Activity 7: this involves analysis of a skill development activity in terms of the modes of learning involved, the cycles which occur, so that re-design can be proposed and tried out.

Activity 8: this involves practice and learning about giving and eliciting feedback.

Activity 9: this involves developing instant interactive case studies.

Activity 10: which involves setting up the 'episodic' method for small group work, described in Chapter 8.

Activity 11: involves setting up the 'stored' method for small group work described in Chapter 9.

These activities are arranged in an order which follows the Chapters 5 to 9. The last two are complete practice runs for the 'episodic' and 'stored' approaches, whereas the earlier activities involve specific elements embodied in the approaches.

From the description they sound rather more complicated than they are in fact. They all involve experimentation with the ideas presented together with feedback to yourself.

ACTIVITY 6: SKILL DEVELOPMENT STRATEGIES

Process

1. Look at a skill development activity you are familiar with.
2. Identify what is going on, and the learning strategy being used.
3. Suggest ways of modifying the situation.
4. Try these out and evaluate the result.

1. Looking at a skill development activity

The activity should preferably be one which you have run as a facilitator, either by yourself or with someone else. It could be that you would prefer to base the activity on a learning situation that you have experienced as a learner. This may shed a different light on the situation, but might make it impossible to proceed with step 4, unless you were going to run a similar activity yourself or can get someone else to make and evaluate the modifications. Ways in which the activity can be 'looked at':

(a) look at a well documented design, at the level of tutor notes. For example, the Pfeiffer and Jones manuals are written at this level of detail (Pfeiffer and Jones, 1975); or
(b) if you are running the event, video record the whole session with a fixed camera, particularly ensuring that _you_ do not move outside camera range; or
(c) sit in while someone else runs the session and analyse as the session proceeds; or
(d) make notes and observations of a session you are running.

The most effective for this self-development activity is likely to be (b). I have not found any difficulty with doing this providing the rationale for doing it is adequately explained to the learner group.

2. Identifying what is going on and the strategy being used

One source of data for analysing the situation will

be your own observation, but of prime importance will be data from the learners if this is obtainable (this is likely to be a weakness of 1 (a) above). A suitable questionnaire would be based on open-ended questions of the type which follow.

LEARNER QUESTIONNAIRE (POST-EVENT)

Q.1   Name of session:

Q.2   Name of learner:

Q.3   You may have learned some new information, facts, knowledge or new ideas, theories or gained insights:

         Please say what you have learned from this session:

         What helped you to learn?

Q.4   You may have learned some new skills and be able to <u>do</u> something which you have not been able to do before, or you may have enhanced an ability you already had to some degree:

Please say what you learned to do from this session:

What helped you to learn?

Q.5   You may have experienced new feelings, or recognised feelings you have had for some time:

Please say what you learned from this session

What helped you to learn?

Q.6   How did you feel about the session?

Q.7   Are there any other comments you would
           like to make about the session?

This information will be treated as confidential.
Thank you for your help. (Please return to:
....
....)
_____

RATIONALE BEHIND QUESTIONNAIRE DESIGN

(a)   the learner is encouraged to report cognitive
       skill and affective learning by using 3
       questions about learning, one identified with
       each category. This will indicate some sort of
       balance (or lack of it). Answers are sometimes
       recorded in the wrong place, but overall a
       wider range of answers seems to result than be
       asking a single question.

(b)   The 'what have you learned' question allows
       the learner to respond in any way (s)he likes.
       This is very important for analysis because
       the form of the answer gives clues to a number
       of factors. For example, a learner who
       answers Q.3 by a statement like 'that manpower
       planning is difficult' appears to have learned
       very little, but may have acquired or
       reinforced a negative attitude towards the

subject. In contrast, a learner who answers
Q.4 by a statement such as 'I now feel
confident that I can handle a disciplinary
interview even if the person concerned is
difficult' seems not only to have learned some
new skill, but appears to have closed the loop
with reflective learning. I realise that this
does not guarantee that the learner can in
fact perform in the back home situation, which
raises issues concerned with evaluation
technology. Clearly if on-the-job evaluation
can be done this would give a much more
reliable measure, but might require more
effort than could reasonably be invested in a
self-development activity. Asking the learner
to identify what helped the learning will
supplement other data about what facilitated
the learning.

(c) The last two questions tap other data which
may give further insight into 'what's going
on'. It should be remembered that deep level
significant learning may be accompanied by
bad feelings (Snell and Binsted, 1981).

<u>Analysis of the data</u> (learner and your own
observation)

Separate out the 3 elements of the development
strategy under the following headings using the work
pages which follow.

RAISING AWARENESS

Evidence of raising negative awareness	What caused this?

Evidence of raising positive awareness	What caused this?

DEVELOPING THE ABILITY TO ACT

Evidence that learning has taken place	What caused this?

HOW WERE THE SKILLS DEFINED?

From research findings? (Tick as appropriate)

                                              Yes   No

From the experience of the learners or tutor?

                                              Yes   No

From experimentation within the learning
activity?

                                              Yes   No

Were skills being worked on at level 3? Any
comments.

3. Suggest ways of modifying the situation

Look at the evidence and your analysis of what
caused it, and suggest modifications which might
get a better balance of learning, strengthen weak
parts of the design, or just try something
different which in your view should work better
(you should know why you think it should be
'better')

4. Try out and evaluate

This in effect takes you back to step 1. The learner questionnaire data is your real source of feedback in this activity which I am sure you will have identified as a discovery-reflective cycle of your learning.

END OF ACTIVITY 6

ACTIVITY 7 MODES OF LEARNING AND LEARNING CYCLES
(CHAPTER 6 IS RELEVANT)

Process

1. Analyse a skill development activity from the point of view of the design of the learning cycle.
2. Analyse what happened from observation and learner data.
3. Suggest re-design which would make the event more whole-cycle.
4. Try out and evaluate.

1. Analysing the design of a skill development activity

The options for looking at an activity (1a-d) suggested in Activity 6 are relevant. In this case a documented design is equally effective. Identify the cycles of learning identifiable in the design, and record the sequences. This should give a clear picture of the intention of the designer.

2. Analysing the outworking of the design

A video recording will again be best, but sitting-in or making notes may suffice. The learner questionnaire from Activity 6 will provide vital learner data. For a self-development exercise this data is vital since this is the only way to find out what is going on inside the learner. Thus the design of the activity may suggest that the learners should be involved in a discovery cycle, but whether any or all of them are actually going through such a cycle is another question. As in Activity 6 the phrasing of the responses to the questions will give clues to which modes of learning contribute to which learning outcomes, feelings, etc.

Collect the questionnaire data together under the following headings.

RECEPTION OF INPUT

Learning reported   Reported source of
                                     learning

_____

DISCOVERY

Learning reported   Reported source of
                                     learning

_____

REFLECTION

Learning reported	Reported source of learning

3. Suggest re-design

The next steps are:

(a)   to link the learning reported by the learners
      with the three modes of learning, thus
      building up your own model of the event;
(b)   to re-design the activity to accomplish more
      whole cycle learning or cycles in a different
      order.

4. Try out and evaluate

The re-design can be tried out and evaluated,
preferably by you, which in effect takes you back
through this activity again.

END OF ACTIVITY 7

ACTIVITY 8 GENERATING FEEDBACK

Process

1. Video record yourself giving/eliciting feedback.
2. Analyse your behaviour.
3. Draw your own conclusions.
4. Modify your methods and again video record.

This activity should help you to develop your skill, solo. If you can work with a colleague there would be considerable advantage and the process suggested here could be modified. Assuming solo practice:

1. Video recording yourself giving/eliciting feedback during a skill development activity

This can be done with a fixed camera, when you are working with a group, so long as you do not move off camera (see comments for Activity 6).

2. Analyse behaviour

This can be done straight off a replay of the video. Analyse your behaviour into giving and eliciting and then designate this as successful/not successful. This can be done to some extent by observation but much better by collecting data from learners using the learner questionnaire suggested in Activity 6. In identifying each episode where you are giving/eliciting feedback either index the tape so you can find them again, or use the analysis sheet on the next work page, to capture key phrases you used.

3. Draw conclusions

Look at your analysis and see if you can identify the elements that were present in the successful episodes (preferably those associated with positive evidence of learning with details of what sort of learning it was). Think through some of the implications of Chapter 6. How dependant are you making the learner? How evaluative is your feedback? How are you focusing the learning down at level 3?

4. Modifying your methods

Think of some ways of modifying your behaviour and try these out repeating the cycle of learning already used. As you add to the analysis sheet on the work page you will again be building up a collection of ideas and behaviours that work for you.

ANALYSIS SHEET FOR GIVING/ELICITING FEEDBACK

Phrases used	Success-ful/un-success-full	Dependant/independant	Notes
Giving feedback			
Eliciting feedback			

Conclusions

END OF ACTIVITY 8

ACTIVITY 9 INSTANT INTERACTIVE CASE STUDIES

Process

1. Generate an 'instant interactive case study' from your own personal experience.
2. Gather at least one other person and generate one from them.
3. Get them to reproduce the interaction.
4. Draw any conclusions you feel appropriate.

The latter part of Chapter 7 is relevant.

1. Generating from your own experience

This part of the activity is to help you experience from the learner's point of view, what it is like to be asked to develop an 'instant case study'. Here is a way of doing it.

(a) Think of a situation where you interact with some other person, where the interaction is not satisfactory from your point of view. You might find the interaction a source of frustration, anger, or resentment. It might have a characteristic pattern and happens with one person on several occasions, or it might be a more general situation which happens with different people. It might be that the thing you would like not to happen is associated with a particular situation or context. There should be a desire in you to change the situation in some way.

(b) Try to encapsulate the situation in a few short sentences in notes.

(c) Could you reproduce the interaction with someone else if asked to do so? If not what have you left out of your description?

2. Generating from another person

(a) Get a friend/colleague/volunteer to do what you have just done in (a) above, and to make a few notes.

(b) Ask them to describe the situation verbally in one or two minutes.

(c) Ask any clarifying questions until the situation is clear in your mind.

3. Reproducing the interaction

(a) As soon as you feel you can take the role of the 'other person' in the interaction that your colleague is describing, invite him to reproduce the interaction with you being the 'other person' involved.

(b) After the interaction has run for a few minutes only, stop it and check if it feels authentic or not to the person who described it in the first place. If not then help him to define what is wrong and try again. If it is rated as authentic then you have created an 'instant interactive case study'.

If you have collected more than one other person then you can try to get someone other than yourself to take the role of 'the other person' in the interaction described.

4. Draw any conclusions you feel appropriate

END OF ACTIVITY 9

ACTIVITY 10 THE EPISODIC APPROACH

Process

1. Collect a small group.
2. Set up the interaction and establish the learning process.
3. Evaluate results and review the process.
4. Plan what you want to do next.

1. Collect a small group

A group of between 3 and 5 is a suitable size to start with, 5 being better than 3. Colleagues might be willing to form such a group, to experience and evaluate the approach. Others might like to join since there should be real learning, around issues of their choice (if an 'instant interactive case study' is used).

2. Set up the interaction and learning process

Follow through the steps described in Chapter 8 for a session of at least one hour. Video record the session if possible.

3. Evaluate results

Ask the members of the group to fill in learner questionnaires as described in Activity 6, and analyse the data as before. Review the video recording, looking for the interventions that you made and noting the phrases you used to help the process along. If you can get the group to join in the review, ask them to help by recalling feelings, thoughts etc. after each of your interventions. This uses the principles of stimulated recall (Kagan, 1982).

4. Plan what to do next

There are two options here:

(a) To identify what interventions you want to experiment with or improve, think of ways of doing this and then try them out with the same or a different group.

(b) A more adventurous, but potentially more effective way would be to use the group to suggest modifications to your interventions as you review each episode. This process can then be extended to reproduce the 'stored' method by asking the group to model alternative interventions off the video. This is particularly useful with a group made up of colleagues. What is happening if this is done is that the group are giving you (the facilitator) feedback about your intervention and facilitating behaviour. They can then model alternative behaviour and provide feedback on that, thus using the stored approach off the video.

It could again be useful to keep a record of useful phrases that are effective to build up your repertoire of behaviours that work for you. You may find alternative (b) a little strange to handle as you will be both facilitator and receiver of feedback.

END OF ACTIVITY 10

ACTIVITY 11 THE STORED APPROACH

Process

1. Collect a small group.
2. Set up the interaction and establish the learning process.
3. Evaluate the results and review the process.
4. Plan what you want to do next.

Proceed in the same manner as for Activity 10, but this time base the session on the 'stored' approach described in Chapter 9. If you can get the group to review your interventions and facilitating behaviour with you, this will be a further opportunity to practise the 'stored' approach, with yourself as the receiver of feedback.

You will, of course, need two sets of video equipment. You will be videoing yourself using the video in the stored approach.

END OF ACTIVITY 11

11 Informal approaches and group coaching

An approach for informal interpersonal skill
development with a group where the facilitator
is most often the manager acting as the coach.

INTRODUCTION

In Chapters 8 and 9 two approaches were described
in some detail, which utilised the various
principles already developed, of whole cycle
learning etc.. These two approaches can be used in
the context of off the job training in conjunction
with different sorts of vehicles like structured
experiences, role plays or instant interactive case
studies. They both are based on the fact that
there is a learner group and facilitator, though as
has already been suggested, once a group gets used
to the process little or no tutor support may be
required. To some extent both the 'episodic' and
the 'stored' approach are formalised with a learner
group in an overtly learning situation, as in say a
workshop. The approaches described in this and the
subsequent Chapter are for informal learning
situations.

INFORMAL APPROACHES

Informal approaches are described as suitable for on the job training and development and can be used spontaneously over very short time spans (although longer sessions are equally suitable if available). Significant learning can be achieved from short sessions if handled skilfully. The advantage of informal approaches is that they can be switched into (or out of) quickly with little or no preparation, in the context of a meeting, discussion, or a debriefing after an interaction has taken place. The theme of this Chapter is that notwithstanding the informality of the situation, the activity still needs to be designed as a complete learning activity, using the principles already referred to.

COACHING

One word often associated with on the job learning is coaching. For example, Singer defines coaching as:

> Seeking to help a man to find solutions to work problems (Singer 1981).

This definition assumes coaching is done by a manager with a subordinate. There is no logical reason why a trainer should not coach. Coaching generally assumes a one to one activity (Megginson and Boydell, 1981), but the use of group coaching can have great advantage particularly for the development of interpersonal skills. The informal approaches described in this and the subsequent Chapter, can be described as 'coaching' where the goal is to increase people's ability to behave effectively. The skill in this form of coaching is to informally create whole cycle learning either in a group or a one to one situation. This involves creating a situation which contains action, feedback, modelling, and reflection.

GROUP COACHING

There are certain advantages to be gained from

developing interpersonal skills in a small group of people. An example will now be described, incorporating the principles already discussed, where the coach (facilitator) is the manager. The session starts with a manager and a small group (2-6) of his subordinates (salesmen) meeting to discuss problems and learn how to improve their selling skills, by focusing on the salesman's behaviour with the customer.

1. Identifying Problems

The manager asks everyone to think of their current sales campaign, and a face to face interaction with a customer which they have found difficult or would like to improve. He asks them to identify the situation and individually make a few notes of the details.

2. Selecting the Problems

When this is done they share (1 minute each) what each person has written. (This is developing an 'instant interactive case study'.) The manager checks for similarity of the situations and generalises if that is helpful, i.e. pulls out common themes. The group then chooses which problem to work on, as quickly as possible, by concentrating on a problem that people 'own' and have energy to work on. This identifies the 'situation of action' and the behaviour which is thought to be ineffective.

3. Describing the Interaction

The manager then asks the person who identified the problem to describe the situation in more detail as illustrated in Figure 11.1.

(P = salesman who has identified problem;
C = customer involved in problem (who is of course
not present in the group);
A, B, & D = other members of the group (salesmen);
M = manager)

Managing   Describing   Listening
Process   Situation to   and
                  Rest of Group   Questioning
                                      to
                                      Understand
                                      Situation

Figure 11.1

This clarifies the problem and begins to explore
effective/ineffective behaviour.

4. Replay the Interaction

The manager then checks if someone could <u>take</u> the
role of the customer (avoiding saying <u>play</u> the
role) and then sets up the interaction and gets it
going so that the interaction 'P' has described is
'replayed' as indicated in Figure 11.2.

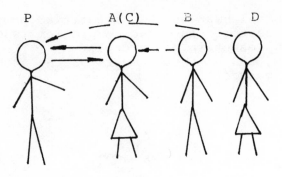

M	P	A(C)	B	D

Setting up
and managing the
process

Interacting, 'P'
replaying problem.
'A' taking role of
customer

Observing

Figure 11.2

This models the problem and makes the 'dimensions
of ability' (or lack of these) visible.

5. Check for Accuracy

The manager stops the process after a short time and
checks if it is accurate. (Is the difficulty being
demonstrated?) Then if <u>not</u> very accurate, he sets
it up again, possibly with someone else being the
customer (remodelling the problem). If accurate he
proceeds to step 6.

6. Generating Feedback

The manager then generates feedback for 'P' by
picking up data, feelings etc., from the group,
being careful to ask people to contribute in an
order which minimises contamination of data
(referred to in Chapter 8). This is shown
diagrammatically in Figure 11.3.

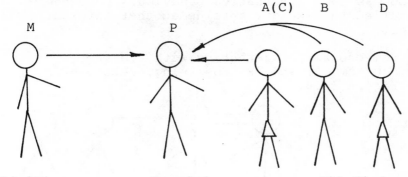

A(C)   B   D

M   P

Eliciting or   Receiving   All Giving
Giving Feed-   Feedback   Feedback
back

Figure 11.3

At this point a number of different learning
processes may be going on in different learners,
e.g. learner 'B' could have received a skill input
by watching 'P' model a particular behaviour.   'P'
will have gone through a discovery loop of action
followed by feedback. Overall this is the
Awareness Raising stage of learning where the
'dimensions of ability' are being explored. It is
important that the discussion and feedback are
about 'dimensions of ability' even if the
'effective behaviour' is also being challenged.
The focus on 'dimensions of ability' can be
achieved by the manager giving feedback of the type
'I noticed "A" became more defensive when you said
...'. Alternatively feedback of this type can be
elicited from the group by questions like 'Did
anyone notice how 'B' reacted when you said ...' or
'What did "P" do to make "B" close up'.

7. Generating Ideas about Alternative Behaviour

The manager now asks for __alternative__ behaviour.
E.g. 'Can anyone think of another way of doing it?'
'How would __you__ do it John?', etc.. This is
utilising the important principle of searching for
ideas for alternative behaviour from the group.

129

8. Model Alternative Behaviour

As soon as some alternative behaviours have been identified the manager sets up another interaction either.

(a) Someone else interacting with the same 'customer', and 'P' observing, as shown in Figure 11.4.

 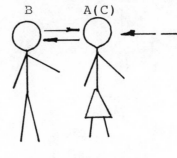 

Setting   Interacting. 'A'   Observing
up and   keeps role of
managing   customer, 'B'
process   is the salesman

Figure 11.4

OR

(b) Reverse roles of first interaction as shown in Figure 11.5.

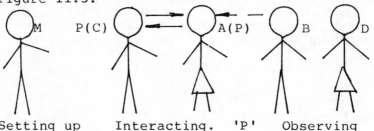

Setting up   Interacting. 'P'   Observing
and managing   takes role of
process   customer, 'A'
               takes role of
               salesperson, 'P'

Figure 11.5

130

Again there are a number of different processes which may be going on in different learners. In 8a, 'P' will be receiving a skill input from 'A's' modelling (as will 'D'), while 'A' and 'B' will be going through the action part of a discovery cycle. The vital part of the process is that 'dimensions of ability' are again visible, which is the reason why the approach is so effective for skill development.

The manager then repeats steps 6, 7 and 8 as often as needed, on the same interaction within the time available, keeping up a good pace.

9. Re-Modelling

(a)   The manager lets the salesman who raised the problem, 'P', reflect on the different ways of interacting which he has seen modelled and then decides how <u>he</u> wants to do it.

(b)   The manager then invites 'P' to do it again but differently from the first time based on the models he has seen, as shown in Figure 11.6.

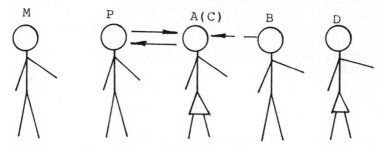

M	P	A(C)	B	D

Setting up   'P' <u>replays</u> the   Observe
and managing   interaction but
process   trying a <u>new</u>
                       behaviour, but is
                       'himself' doing it
                       <u>his</u> way. 'A' takes
                       role of customer

Figure 11.6

This should always be the last step before moving on to work on another problematical interaction.

This step can be achieved very easily by saying something like, 'take a few minutes to consider the situation and then decide how _you_ would like to do it, and then try it again'.

For 'P' this is the final reflective cycle which closes off his whole cycle learning.

Other examples could be given involving say negotiating skills, where the content, roles and skills would be different, but the learning process would follow the same general form.

The reason why genuine skill development takes place is because the learners experience new behaviour either by seeing someone demonstrate it, or by doing it themselves or being on the receiving end on an interaction. Feedback is an essential element of this learning. It is important to realize, however, that sophisticated face to face skills are highly individual. A learner may see a very skilled performance, but cannot reproduce it in exactly the same way, because she is a different person. One key step in skill development is thus the 'personalising' of skill. (An aspect of reflective learning.) This is why step 9 is so important.

SUMMARY OF THE GROUP COACHING PROCESS

1. Get individuals to identify problem interactions.
2. Select and clarify a problem to work on.
3. Describe the interaction in enough detail.
4. Set up the interaction to 'replay' the situation.
5. Check if accurate — no —
   yes   Repeat
6. Generate feedback.
7. Encourage ideas about alternative behaviours.
8. Restart an alternative interaction.
9. Get person who initiated the interaction to try it again, but differently.

132

The reader at this point will be aware that this group coaching process has many similarities with the more formal 'episodic' approach. The principles enshrined in both approaches are the same, and the differences can be summarised in Table 1.

TABLE 1

INFORMAL (coaching)	FORMAL (structured)
Set in informal context of a meeting, chat or debrief after an event	Set in the context of a course, workshop, etc.
Manager as facilitator	Teacher/trainer as facilitator
Based on problem or difficulty encountered	Based on skill areas covered by course goals
Deals with episodes and specific areas for improvement	Deals with whole interaction, episode by episode
No pre-planning, take what comes up	Pre-planned both by trainer and learners

It is self evident that in an informal situation, where learning will be occurring in a work situation (such as a meeting), video recording of the original situation will not be available and it is assumed that video will not be involved in the coaching session. Thus an equivalent to the 'stored' approach does not exist.

SOME VARIATIONS

There are a number of variations from the approach just described.

(a) A manager (acting as facilitator) may play a much more directive part and get the group to work on a problem of <u>his</u> choice. These may be problems he feels his people have, but do not recognise. Experience indicates there is still a need to get 'ownership' of the problem by the group. Alternatively the manager may need to direct the groups attention to new problems which will occur in the future, e.g. 'we need to work out how to cope with this new situation which none of us have experienced before'. This could be most important in situations of change.

(b) Again using a sales example, the group can be used to explore problems involving more than one customer or more than one salesman. All this requires is to set up the interaction allocating the appropriate roles, e.g. one salesman and a group of three customers, as illustrated in Figure 11.7.

Managing process

Interacting. 'P' being himself

'A', 'B' & 'D' taking the role of customer group

Figure 11.7

Mention has already been made about the informality of this approach. A group coaching session may be integrated into a meeting for a short period to explore a problem, and then the rest of the agenda can be resumed. Clearly there is a spectrum from formal to informal, and a group coaching session may be formalised until it becomes a miniture workshop. This Chapter focuses on the most informal versions of group coaching.

FACILITATING THE LEARNING

Some useful rules

1. 'Minimise discussion, maximise the action'. Although verbal feedback, description and discussion are important elements in the learning process, it is the action which helps the group forward the most, for two reasons.

   (a) Action helps the group to focus and recognise the 'dimensions of ability' (Level 3).
   (b) Getting some pace into the proceedings is particularly important in these informal situations. With practice the process can be very fast and several cycles gone through in 15 minutes.

This leads to the second rule:

2. As soon as anyone shows any sign of having an alternative behaviour get them into action. For example, a learner may say 'I don't think Betty put enough emphasis on the benefits'. Without seeking further verbal clarification the manager could say 'Right, could you take over the interview and see if you can do that' or 'show us what you mean'. If nobody in the group seems to be verbalising any alternative behaviour, progress can be made by asking someone else to 'do it the way you normally do it'. It is usually much more productive to compare two ways of doing something than debating one at length.

3. Check informally if people feel they have

learned anything. Get them to write it down first and then share afterwards. This gives the coach information about where people have got to and helps the reflective process.

Although all these rules apply to the more formal approaches they are particularly vital for the informal approaches.

The principle being used in this approach is to get the behaviour acted out, so that it can be experienced and observed as well as discussed. It is this aspect which stimulates genuine skill development. Without this, learning is likely to be restricted to knowing what <u>not</u> to do, or better, knowing what <u>should</u> be done, but it does <u>not</u> follow that a person <u>will</u> be <u>able</u> to do it. The approach described concentrates on helping people to <u>be able</u> to interact more effectively.

<u>Handling the Feedback</u>

As for the formal approaches described in Chapter 8 and 9, the facilitator (manager) needs to elicit feedback from different people in the group since they will have different feedback to give. So in our example, the manager can ask the person taking the role of the customer how <u>she</u> feels about the approach (on the receiving end). He can ask the person taking the role of the salesman how he thinks the interview is going. He can ask the observers for their views. He can also, of course, give feedback himself, but Barnard emphasizes the advantage of facilitating feedback from learners as a way of minimising some of the problems associated with facilitator feedback. He cites some undesirable features of facilitator feedback as:

> critical, subjective, inappropriate, incomparable, incomprehensive, prescriptive, and excessive. (Barnard, 1980)

He suggests the facilitator has some authority in the situation 'either assumed, expected or inherent' (Barnard, 1980). In the case of an informal coaching session run by the boss (manager) the authority is very real. The most appropriate

climate for the facilitator to encourage when the
skills are complex and sophisticated (as with
managers and professional people) is one of
exploration and experimentation.

SUMMARY

Informal approaches to interpersonal skill
development, which can be used on the job are
identified as 'coaching'. The process for
establishing group coaching can be integrated in
other activities by the manager of a group. A key
rule of thumb is to 'minimise the discussion and
maximise the action', and establish a climate of
exploration and experiment.

12 One to one coaching

Using the principles of whole cycle learning
when the coach is working with only one
learner and has been present at a real live
interaction.

INTRODUCTION

One to one coaching involves just two people. This
is the more usual meaning of the word coaching. The
advantage is that it can be done immediately
following a real life interaction where the coach
has been present. Thus there is no need to set up
a problem, since the vehicle for the session is
behaviour which has just taken place, and been
observed by the coach. The disadvantage is that
there is no flow of ideas or demonstrations of
alternative behaviour from a group, and the sources
of feedback are thus reduced. In general the
session from the coaches' point of view is more
difficult to run. However, having said that the
advantages can outweigh the disadvantages providing
the facilitator develops appropriate skills, because
it may immediately follow a real life interaction.

THE ONE TO ONE PROCESS

Let us take the example of a Personnel Officer who
has just completed a negotiation with a Shop
Steward with his boss present. The boss was not
taking a major part in the interaction, but
immediately the Shop Steward has gone, the boss
starts a coaching session. The principles involved
are the same as for group coaching.

The process is as follows:

1. Agreeing the Agenda

The boss identifies an agenda with the Personnel
Officer - 'What do we want to work on?', 'Which bits
did you find difficult or uncomfortable?'. This
acknowledges the principle of 'ownership'. He may
put in some suggestions himself.

2. Getting into Action

The boss takes an episode or incident during the
interview, discusses it and then either replays it
or suggests alternative behaviour by getting into
action as shown diagrammatically in Figures 12.1
and 12.2.

B = Boss
S = Shop Steward (not present)
P = Personnel Officer

There are only two alternatives:

Either:
(a)

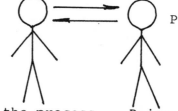

B(S)   P

Setting up and managing the process,   Being
but also taking the part of the   himself
Shop Steward   in the
                                interaction

Figure 12.1

OR
(b)

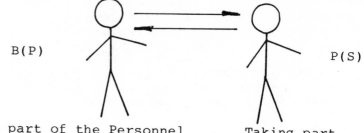

B(P)   P(S)

Taking the part of the Personnel   Taking part
Officer   of the Shop
                                           Steward

Figure 12.2.

3. Generating Feedback

The boss generates feedback, only in this case
there are only two sources, the Personnel Officer
and himself.

4. Develops Ideas for Alternative Behaviour

The boss gets suggestions for alternative behaviour
or suggests alternatives himself. Repeat steps
2-4.

5. Replay in Original Role

The last step of getting the Personnel Officer to
practice new behaviour 'his way' is an important
step in closing the learning cycle and raising
confidence. See Figure 12.3.

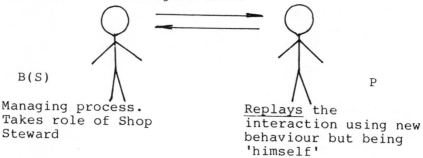

B(S)   P

Managing process.   Replays the
Takes role of Shop   interaction using new
Steward   behaviour but being
                               'himself'

Figure 12.3

When both are satisfied that a new behaviour has been acquired they move on to another episode from the agenda. As can be seen this process has similarities with group coaching, but requires the coach not only to manage the learning process, but engage in the interaction, recall what happened in the original interaction, and give feedback. This is why it is more difficult to do. This approach can be used in 'curbstone coaching' already referred to.

The <u>process</u> may be summarised as follows:

1. ┌ Identifying the agenda and selecting problems
2. ┌┤ Get into action.
3. │├ Generate feedback.   Repeat
4. │└▸Develop suggestions for alternative behaviour.
5. └▸ Let the subordinate personalise the feedback
     and try out a new behaviour.
                                    Repeat

It is possible to move quickly from on stage to the other, and the suggested rules for group coaching are equally relevant for one to one coaching. Pace may be generated by suggestions such as – Boss: 'Let me try and show you what you might have done, I'll be you ...'.

Role reversal will quite often occur simply because there are only two people involved. Modelling (receiving a skill input) discovery and reflective learning will often follow in quick succession.

THE COACHING ROLE

These observations apply to both group and one to one coaching. In any of these situations the coach may choose what sort of role to adopt. She may be highly directive choosing topics to work on, giving evaluative feedback, reinforcing good behaviour, pointing out faults, etc. Alternatively, she may be very non-directive, exploring areas of concern of the learner, working off his/their agenda, eliciting non-evaluative feedback from the group, exploring options with the group and joining in the learning herself. The approach does not prescribe the way in which the facilitator operates. There

are, however, consequences depending on this
choice, and these will be discussed in Chapter 16.
In the one to one version there is some problem
with what role the coach will play during the real
interview. Ideally he may wish to say nothing and
take notes, but this may not be acceptable to the
other party (e.g. customer, Shop Steward)
especially if he is the boss. This part of
the interaction may need careful pre-planning and
discussion before the event. A situation to be
avoided is for the boss to take over the
interaction, since this effectively destroys the
learning opportunity unless the boss only wants to
'show him how to do it'.

THE SKILLS OF COACHING

Singer has an impressive list of characteristics
required to perform effective coaching, which is
based on developing knowledge (cognitive learning).
There would appear to be a parallel but slightly
different set of characteristics associated with
coaching for skill development. For example,
Singer's 'uses examples from similar situations'
might be translated into 'demonstrates alternative
behaviour from his own experience'. The skills of
coaching listed by Singer are:

    Observation
    Listening
    Appraisal
    Discussion
    Delegation
    (Singer, 1981).

    Again these are appropriate to understanding and
cognitive learning. In coaching for interpersonal
skill development the key skills appear to be
somewhat different, e.g.

    * Developing ownership of problems or issues to
    be worked on
    * Setting up the interactions fast and
    informally.
    * Giving or eliciting feedback of the appropriate
    type.
    * Helping to define the 'dimensions of ability'.

* Managing the learning process particularly
focusing down to 'dimensions of ability'.
* Helping others to demonstrate alternative
behaviours or do this himself.
* Helping learners to try it for themselves in
the session and back on the job.

THE BALANCE OF LEARNING

Phillips and Fraser discuss the three different
approaches to interpersonal skill training of
thinking, doing and feeling. They make the point
that

> I.S.T. does not have to be either "thinking" or
> "doing" or "feeling" in its scope but can
> involve all three with different emphasis as
> required. (Phillips and Fraser, 1982)

This links in with the ideas of holistic
and composite learning introduced in Chapter 2. In
the approaches described in this and the previous
Chapter, the emphasis has been on 'doing'
activities with 'thinking' and 'feeling' stemming
from real life problems and set-up interactions.
The more important consideration is 'What sort of
learning takes place?'. In a productive session of
the type described it is likely that thinking,
doing, and feeling learning will <u>all</u> take place, and
I take the view that it is highly disfunctional for
this to be inhibited. The quality of a coaching
session of the types described can be judged fom
the balance of learning across <u>all three areas</u>.
The overall goal of a coaching session is that <u>new
behaviours have been learned in which the learner
has confidence</u>. The extent of learning will depend
on such things as the feedback strategy adopted
(see Chapter 14), the skill of the coach etc..

CONCLUSIONS

The advantage of informal coaching approaches
described are that they:

(a)   build from learners' experience and problems;
(b)   can be used in many normal work situations,

e.g. at normal staff meetings, after on the job interactions, etc.'

(c) can be done in quite short time slots, e.g. 30 minutes;

(d) produce genuine skill development;

(e) need no other resources;

(f) involve whole cycle learning (modelling, discovery and reflection).

The key to success lies in the coach being able to design and run sessions as learning processes.

SUMMARY

One to one coaching sessions can be set up using the same principles of whole cycle learning. These sessions would normally follow a live interaction at which the coach is present. The coach has to not only manage the process, but get involved in interactions, generate feedback and recall what happened in the original interaction. This actually makes it more difficult to do, but has the advantage of working off a real life interaction.

13 Self development activities covering chapters 11 and 12

These activities are designed to help you to explore the setting up and running of informal approaches to interpersonal skill development using group and one to one coaching.

INTRODUCTION

Since the coach may be a manager rather than a trainer, it may be that you are wanting to train managers to handle these approaches (if you are a trainer). If this is the case Activity 15 and 16 give some guidance on how to do this. It is strongly recommended that you practice doing it yourself before you try to train others. It would also be an advantage to finish reading the monograph before attempting Activities 15 and 16.

MENU OF ACTIVITIES

Activity 12, this is to help you move from discussion into action informally in a meeting or other work situation.

<u>Activity 13</u>, is to practice the group coaching approach.

<u>Activity 14</u>, is to practice the one to one coaching approach.

After reading the rest of the monograph:

<u>Activity 15</u>, is a design for training others in group coaching.

<u>Activity 16</u>, is a design for training others in one to one coaching.

ACTIVITY 12 INTRODUCING ACTION INFORMALLY INTO A WORK SITUATION

Process

1. Select a meeting or other work activity where it would be natural to talk about interpersonal skills.
2. Get the group into action.
3. Continue discussing the issue.
4. Repeat stages 2 and 3.
5. Collect your phrases and note effect.

1. Select a work activity

Any meeting that you regularly attend or can legitimately set up or any informal discussion about some interaction involving interpersonal skill will do. For this activity any number of people will be adequate. Thus one other person will do. It would be very helpful to take an audio recording of the proceedings.

2. Get into action

Do not explain to the group what you are going to do. This may sound strange, but in my experience the more you explain the more problems seem to arise. This breaks a rule that I normally follow of being very open about the rationale for workshop and learning event designs. In this case the more explanation is given, the more the process sounds complicated and unfamiliar and the group gets more and more apprehensive about starting. This is particularly the case in the informal approaches where just the opposite reaction is required. Not saying anything has the added advantage that no one will notice if it does not work first time round. The ideal way is to 'flip' the group into action without any one really noticing. For example, if someone is talking about a problem they have with Fred, say something like 'I can't quite home in on the issue here, what do you actually say to him?' When he responds continue 'Hang on, let me be Fred, then say it to me'. You can then respond in an appropriate way and continue the interaction or just comment, or give some feedback, 'I feel very put down by the way you said that'.

3. Continue discussion

Of course at this point you could go into a full coaching session but for this activity merely continue the discussion.

4. Repeat stages 2 and 3

Take another opportunity to get the group into action again.

5. Collect your phrases

Listen to the tape recording after the session is over and note useful phrases you used and begin to list any useful rules you can think of, on the work page provided.

Phrases that produced action in the group	Phrases or statements that did not produce action in the group

Rules which are emerging:

END OF ACTIVITY 12

ACTIVITY 13 PRACTICE A GROUP COACHING SESSION

Process

1. Get group together.
2. Set up group coaching session and establish learning process.
3. Evaluate the results and review the process.
4. Plan what you want to do next.

1. Get the group together

As for Activity 10 a group of 3 to 5 would be ideal. But in this instance the group would need to meet around some work activity where it is legitimate for interpersonal skills to be discussed. If this is difficult for any reason then an ad hoc group could be set up and people asked to identify particular personal problems they may have that they would like to work on. The problem with this latter is that what is being set up is very close to the more formal 'episodic' approach which was the subject of Activity 10. As with Activity 12, it will be better not to say anything to the group about your intentions. The key issue is whether interpersonal skills are a legitimate part of the meeting or can be easily made so.

2. Set up coaching session

Following the process described for group coaching introduce a cycle of activity around at least one issue. Video tape your activities if at all possible.

3. Evaluate the results and review the process

This may present problems, since the use of the learner questionnaire would not seem very appropriate in an informal situation. A possibility would be to pick up data from the group immediately after a cycle of coaching. One group I worked with established the habit of summarising what they felt should be done about a problem on a flip chart. Informal conversation with members of the group would also be appropriate and should produce some element of evaluation. Look at the video for the interventions that you made, capturing useful phrases that work, and phrases that did not produce useful learning or action. An example might be where you invited someone to 'see if she could improve on that' which resulted in a refusal to do so. Again start forming your own set of rules that fit your own culture.

4. Plan what you want to do next

Decide what you need to do next to improve your coaching skills.

EVALUATION SHEET

Phrases or interventions that worked	Phrases or interventions that did not work

Rules which are emerging:

END OF ACTIVITY 13

ACTIVITY 14 PRACTICE A ONE TO ONE COACHING SESSION

Process

1. Observe an interaction between two or more people.
2. Set up a one to one coaching session.
3. Evaluate the results and review the process.
4. Plan what you want to do next.

1. Observe an interaction

Ideally use a situation to which you have easy entry. If you are a trainer, sitting in on a colleague's session would be ideal, since training is a sophisticated interpersonal skill. Access to other work situations would be required as an alternative. If you are a manager then observing a colleague or subordinate would be ideal. In either case it would be necessary to negotiate time for the coaching session which would follow without giving any significant detail about the process. It is also important to have an understanding about your role during the interaction itself, which should be the minimum possible. For example, sitting in on another trainer's session may allow no involvement whatsoever. However, a visit to a customer may require some involvement for politeness sake, particularly if you are the boss. It is, of course, vital that interpersonal skills are a key element in the situation.

2. Set up a one to one coaching session

Follow the process for one to one coaching given in Chapter 12. Run a session for 30 minutes and video record if possible.

3. Evaluate the results

Since the coaching session only involves one other person and is in private, it would be quite feasible to use the learner questionnaire from Activity 6. The person coached could be involved in giving you feedback, and he could coach you by using aspects of the 'stored' approach off video. Again it is suggested that you use the evaluation sheet and begin developing your own rules. In this activity the data should be more objective.

4. Plan what you want to do next

As before.

EVALUATION SHEET

Phrases or interventions that worked	Phrases or interventions that did not work

Rules which are emerging:

END OF ACTIVITY 14

ACTIVITY 15 RUNNING A GROUP COACHING SKILLS SESSION FOR MANAGERS

Process

1. Set up a group.
2. Make some introductory inputs.
3. Demonstrate a group coaching session.
4. Explain the process the group has just experienced.
5. Ask them to set up their own group coaching session.
6. Use the 'stored' approach to facilitate their learning.

1. Set up the group

The purpose of this activity is to train a small group of people to use group coaching. You will act as facilitator. Clearly this is not a complete design for a skill development workshop, but this activity focuses on using the more formal approach described in Chapter 9 to begin the process of developing coaching skills in others. You need to be proficient in using both the group coaching approach and the 'stored' approach before attempting this activity. You will need a group of between 4 and 6. It might feel safer to select a group of colleagues rather than a group of managers if you are a trainer or educator.

2. Make some introductory inputs

Some input about the purpose of the activity and what interpersonal skills are will probably be required, but I advise <u>not</u> explaining the group coaching process at this point, because according to the principles already presented it will be much more effective to demonstrate it.

3. Demonstrate a group coaching session

Run a group coaching session as in Activity 13, including exploring problem interactions identified by the group. It is important that these are real problems owned by group members. Run the session for 45 minutes or so. Make sure you make a variety of interventions and go through several cycles of learning. Since this is a demonstration this needs to go well.

4. Explain the process

Show the group the learning process they have gone through using diagrams and explain what is going to happen next.

5. Set up and get them to run another session

Ask one of the group to act as coach, and let him go through the whole process of selecting something to work on and then running the session. In the first stage it may be that the coach can use the list of problem interactions identified in the demonstration. The session should continue for 1 hour, and be video recorded. It helps to focus on the coach and to index the tape so that you know exactly where he starts or stops an intervention. Get group members to record any learning from the session.

6. Using the stored approach

Using the stored approach described in Chapter 9 focus attention only on the interventions and facilitating behaviour used by the coach. Develop feedback (including learning) get the group to model alternative behaviour etc.. This is quite difficult to do first time around, but the practice you have already had in Activity 11 should help. You will need at least 2 hours to work through a 1 hour coaching session. N.B. the rational for doing it this way and comment on this design can be found in Chapter 17.

END OF ACTIVITY 15

ACTIVITY 16 RUNNING A ONE TO ONE COACHING SKILLS SESSION FOR MANAGERS

Process

1. Set up a group.
2. Set up an interaction.
3. Get a group member to set up and run a one to one coaching session.
4. Use the stored approach to facilitate learning.

1. Set up a group

The first point to make is that this activity needs to follow Activity 15, and use only people from the group used for Activity 15. This is because it is more difficult and they need experience of group coaching. For this activity only 3 or 4 people are required.

2. Set up the interaction

Since the group members have experienced the group coaching session it is generally adequate to describe the one to one process and contrast it with the group process. A demonstration by you would be better, but would add 1 hour on to the total time for this activity. Having understood the process it is now necessary for a problematic interaction to be set up where the 'learner' can interact with one or more people and be observed by the 'coach'. Planning how the 'coach' behaves and how she keeps out of the interaction is an important piece of discovery learning. Any spare member of the group can observe. This part of the process does not require video taping. This should last about 30 minutes. The process for this stage can be shown diagrammatically as in Figure 13.1.

  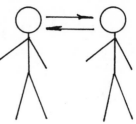

Facilitator   'Coach'   'Learner'
set up   observing   interacting
                                          with 'other'

Figure 13.1

3. Running the coaching session

The coach then runs a one to one coaching session
with the 'learner' for around 30 minutes. The
session will need video taping. The 'learner' can
then be asked to write down what he has learned,
and other members of the group will have been
observers.

4. Using the 'stored' approach

As in Activity 15, use the whole group to model
alternative behaviour, use the learning recorded by
the 'learner' as feedback and generate more about
dimensions of ability. This session will take
about $1\frac{1}{2}$ hours.

END OF ACTIVITY 16

14 Feedback strategies and learning theories

More about feedback, how to look out for
significant sources, the different forms of
feedback and their relation to learning
theories, how to develop a strategy.

FEEDBACK

Now that some of the options for developing
interpersonal skills have been explored, it becomes
clear that a key activity for all the options is
the generation of feedback. In Chapter 6 the
importance of feedback as an element of discovery
learning was emphasised. Reference has also been
made to the options of giving as compared with
eliciting feedback. This is not just an issue of
facilitator control, but of drawing on the
resources of the group, some of whom will have
unique contributions to make. For example, those
involved in an interaction will have different data
from those who observe.

PICKING UP THE 'GOLD BRICKS'

A skill that a facilitator needs for eliciting feedback is one I describe as 'picking up the gold bricks'. In an interaction the facilitator needs to form a view about what feedback might be forthcoming from the learner group and in which member of the group it resides. This is an important element in knowing when to stop an interaction to ensure that too much feedback does not accumulate, nor that it gets lost or goes cold in the sense that the group has an overload of feedback to deal with and finds difficulty in accurately recalling the earlier episodes. The process of spotting who has what sort of feedback to give, is, I often suggest to facilitators like looking for gold bricks in long grass. It requires a careful search and when one is spotted it needs to be picked up and made use of.

IDENTIFYING THE DIFFERENT FORMS OF FEEDBACK

There are a number of quite different forms of feedback which stem from different learning theories. In practice this means that different learning will result, depending on which form of feedback is employed.

A useful way of distinguishing different types of feedback is to associate them with the various learning theories. The many theories of learning have been most usefully grouped by Burgoyne as follows.

Conditioning
Social influence
Information transfer
Cybernetic
Cognitive
Experiential
Pragmatic
(Burgoyne, 1977)

Most of the theories can be identified in the type of feedback found in interpersonal skill development activities. Feedback types can be differentiated as follows.

1. Reinforcement

Feedback is evaluative, describing behaviour as right or wrong, good, bad, helpful, unhelpful. Learning is facilitated by rewarding correct behaviour (positive reinforcement) or punishing incorrect behaviour. Examples of this approach can be found in (Jones, 1980). This type of feedback is an enactment of 'conditioning' theory based on a stimulus-response interpretation of behaviour. The theory suggests positive reinforcement (reward) is more productive than punishment. In practice this means that activities must be simple enough for most learners to get it right rather than wrong, and that difficulty should be increased in small steps. Rewards should be given immediately, which suggests that short cycles of action - feedback are most productive. Behaviour may be modified by this means and the learners may practice the skill until they have 'got it right'. It does not follow that they understand why they have got it right.

Examples of the sort of facilitation which can be used to enact a conditioning theory of learning (facilitator feedback):

"Did you all notice how effectively Joe put the interviewee at ease by saying ...".

(Facilitator eliciting feedback)

"Did Alice succeed in putting the candidate at ease or not?"

2. Group norms

This is similar to reinforcement and is also likely to be evaluative, but feedback is in terms of the correctness of behaviour and is based on the acceptability of that behaviour judged by group norms.

These norms may develop within the learning group (which can happen in laboratory training when certain behaviour may be categorised as, say, 'not open'), or reflect the norms of the organisation in which the learners all work (in for example a company management course). The learning theory

being enacted is 'social influence' and feedback
will be about acceptability or non-acceptability or
appropriateness of behaviour within a cultural
setting. It is often based on concepts of role and
the learning is about matching behaviour to norms
and role expectations.

  Examples of facilitation (facilitator eliciting
feedback from group):

    "How do you think senior management would react
    to Fred's approach?"

(Facilitator giving feedback)

    "I can't see you getting away with that approach
    with our group of Shop Stewards".

3. Data

Feedback is in the form of data or information
about behaviour, it is factual but this does not
necessarily imply being evaluative. It is likely
to be associated with some form of behaviour
analysis such as that developed by Rackham and
Morgan, which identifies certain types of behaviour
(e.g. gate keeping) which may be further defined as
helpful or unhelpful (Rackham and Morgan, 1977).
Data is then collected about how often such
behaviour occurs, who in the group is displaying
high skill at performing it, or which dimensions of
ability are being displayed. This type of feedback
can be elicited by the use of 'instruments', i.e.
questionnaires, rating or other data collection
scales. Many of these are readily available in
areas such as team working, decision making,
problem solving, etc.. In selling, a sales
interview is often broken down into specific stages
and feedback is given on each stage. Each stage is
recalled by a mnemonic. The use of instruments
implies a model of effective behaviour, i.e. the
dimensions chosen generally imply an effective –
ineffective orientation and therefore tend to be
somewhat evaluative. The facilitator may, however,
elicit non-evaluative data of significance from a
group.

If the analysis system is sophisticated, it is often useful to nominate observer roles in a small group activity, in the knowledge that they are subsequently likely to be a rich source of data, whereas the learners involved in the interaction may find it hard to be objective or to analyse their own behaviour. Some useful ways of analysing interactive behaviour are given by Dyer and Giles (Dyer and Giles 1981).

The use of data as feedback is the enactment of 'cybernetic' theories of learning. Learning is facilitated by comparison of behaviour against models. The data must obviously be understandable to the learner who has been involved in the action (otherwise it is not feedback). This frequently means that learners must be familiar with the method of behaviour analysis, the categories, taxonomies or instruments to be used, as pre-cursors to discovery learning. This is not the case if the facilitator 'picks up' data as it becomes visible in the group. This latter type of feedback is appropriate for awareness raising where learners not only need to understand what behaviour categories are, but also how to recognise them when they occur. The second stage of development is of course to learn how to behave effectively in these ways.

Example of facilitation (facilitator eliciting feedback):

> "Now I want you to rate all the scales on the instrument from 1-7, on your own, then we will share our individual scores and see how well you handled that interaction".

(Facilitator giving feedback)

> "I didn't see any empathising behaviour at any point during that interview".

4. Conceptual

This type of feedback is in terms of concepts, ideas or theories, and is based on the view that understanding and concepts, are an important element of skill development. This involves

not only knowing <u>how</u> to do something but <u>why</u> it is
appropriate to do it that way. This type of
feedback enacts a 'cognitive' theory of learning
which suggests that we have understanding of the
whole interaction and in particular of the
interactive behaviour being learned about. This
may be because the concepts are fundamental enough
to be used to interpret a wide variety of activity.
Examples of these sorts of concepts are The
Managerial Grid (Blake and Mouton, 1964), or
Transactional Analysis (Barker and Phillips, 1981;
Morrison and O'Hearne, 1977). Such concepts or
models provide a rationale for acting in a
particular way and are also a basis for generating
feedback. The concept allows the learner to
interpret behaviour with understanding and more
important to re-plan behaviour in a deliberate way.
For example, a learner might get feedback about his
'parent-child' interaction in an interview with a
subordinate. As with the 'data' type of feedback
based on Behaviour Analysis, learners must first
become familiar with the concepts or theories
before use can be made of this type of feedback.

<u>Examples</u> of facilitation involving conceptual
feedback (facilitator giving feedback with video,
leading on to speculation about how to deal with
such a situation).

> "That bit of the interaction I have just shown
> is a beautiful example of the "Why don't you
> yes but" game (Berne 1964). Now how should
> Bill have got out of that? And when we have
> discussed that, we will look at the next bit
> of tape and see what actually happened".

(Facilitator giving feedback)

> "I saw the way you dealt with Joan as
> classical 5.5 behaviour".

5. Feelings

Feedback is expressed as feelings, i.e. learners
say how they felt about an interaction or what
effect the behaviour had on them at a feelings
level. This type of feedback is the enacting of
'experiential' theories of learning.

'Experiential' is used in a narrow sense, since all discovery learning is in a general sense experiential. Experiential learning in the narrow sense implies groups learning from their own behaviour as it happens. The principle involved is that people are sometimes rational, sometimes irrational and always feeling beings like me, with values, prejudices, and attitudes.

In this type of feedback it is general practice to avoid evaluative feedback or feedback which attributes motives. The N.T.L. rules (NTL, 1969), are a very useful guide in this respect. This type of feedback may concern how the learner felt in carrying out a certain behaviour or how he/she felt on the receiving end of someone else's behaviours. Clues about who might have signficant feelings to share can often be spotted by the facilitator by, for example, looking for non-verbal clues like body position (Phillips and Fraser, 1982), or role in the interaction. An example of this is if triads are set up to practice interviewing skills, with an interviewer, an interviewee and an observer. The first two are most likely to have experienced feelings which will enhance learning. (The observer may have more data about behaviour.) Feelings feedback is often very powerful and significant in producing learning because it begins to impinge on people's self concept (their view of themselves) and may for many people begin exchanges between learners which are outside the norms of work group behaviour. In this situation the facilitator not only needs high skill in eliciting or sometimes giving such feedback, but needs to monitor whether individuals can handle feedback of this type.

Examples of facilitating learning through feelings feedback (facilitator eliciting feedback):

"Jane I noticed you look pretty uncomfortable as the negotiation started, could you tell us how you were feeling just then".

(Facilitator giving feedback)

"Well just watching that interview I felt really on edge, that you were going to blow it completely".

6. Behavioural

This is an unual type of feedback and also can be
seen as an enactment of an 'experiential' learning
theory.   It involves putting learners at the
receiving end of behaviour, either like their own
(as in a role reversal situation) or different.
They can then be asked how they experienced it.   An
example may clarify this type of feedback.   Two
people have been involved in an appraisal
interview, set up within a course.   Frank has
interviewed Jean.   The facilitator then suggests
reversing roles as follows:

> "O.k. now I want you Jean to interview Frank
> using the same style as he has just used on
> you. Try and reproduce his behaviour as
> nearly as you can". (Role reversal)

After they have done this

> "Right now Frank how did you experience that,
> being on the receiving end?"

7. Variations

Many types of feedback can be used during one
discovery learning session.   Sometimes in
combination.

Example (facilitator giving feedback).

> "That was one of the best examples of
> adult-adult behaviour I have seen, and it got
> you right out of that difficult situation".

This is reinforcement and conceptual feedback.   A
useful commentary on feedback forms can be found in
W.G. Wyre and Giles, 1981.

WHAT ABOUT A STRATEGY?

Strategy implies deliberation and pre-planning in
that the facilitator deliberately chooses which
sort of feedback is likely to be most effective

to facilitate the sort of skill development required by the learners. The different types of feedback produce different sorts of learning and are based (whether the facilitator realises it or not) on different assumptions about how people learn (which is what distinguishes the learning theories). All feedback types are effective, but can produce different kinds of learning. In choosing, the facilitator needs to know which is the most appropriate for the learners, taking into account what they need to learn and the facilitator's ability to elicit, give and handle that type of feedback. Table 1 summarises and compares what has been explained in the text and suggests some likely learning results.

The linking of feedback types with learning theories gives a conceptual framework from which to work and choose. Clearly a facilitator can be entirely opportunistic (which could be classed as a strategy), but there would seem to be some advantage in planning since some forms of feedback (data and concepts) require pre-learning of the analysis and concepts.

The learner group may also need time together to get used to certain forms of feedback, particularly feelings type and particularly if this is in a coaching situation and the norms of the organisation are not conducive to this. The learner group may discover for itself the value of certain types of feedback. For example, one person in the group may share some powerful feelings data. If this is seen as useful it can often release others to do the same.

It is sometimes the case that facilitators use a form of feedback without being aware of the learning theory they are enacting. This Argyris and Schon would call their 'theory in use' (Argyris and Schon, 1976). Since learning theories make different assumptions and observations about how people learn and indeed are based on different 'models of man' (Burgoyne and Stuart, 1977), if tutors were asked how they thought people learned and what their 'model of man' was, their espoused theories would be revealed. Incongruence between espoused theory and 'theory in use' are common, but

166

TABLE 14.1

TYPE OF FEEDBACK	LEARNING THEORY	EXAMPLES OF FEEDBACK	TYPE OF SKILL DEVELOPMENT LIKELY TO RESULT ASSOCIATED WITH:
Reinforcement	Conditioning	Evaluative, right/wrong, good/bad	The "right" way to behave
Group Norms	Social Influence	Acceptable to culture and role	The way to behave to succeed in this organisation
Data	Cybernetic	Analysis of behaviour instruments, ratings, etc.	Effective behaviours and measures of how effective I am
Conceptual	Cognitive	Theories, models, concepts	What is effective and why, and what I need to do to improve
Feelings	Experiential	Feelings - reactions	Emotional consequences of my behaviour on others and their behaviour on me (reported)
Behavioural	Experiential	Experiencing someone else's behaviour	As above but now felt

it would at least appear desirable that tutors knew
which theory they were enacting with their preferred
form of feedback.

My personal view is that developing an
appropriate strategy which fits the learner group
and the learning required is an important design
decision, whether the skill development activity is
in the formal context of a course or workshop, or
an informal coaching session.

As far as the skill of the facilitator is
involved, I would argue that he/she should be
competent at handling all forms of feedback and know
under what conditions each is appropriate.

SUMMARY

Feedback is a vital part of an interpersonal skill
development activity. The tutor needs to be aware
of what feedback resides in which member of the
learner group, and needs to 'pick it up'. The
different forms of feedback correspond to different
theories of learning, and are reinforcement, group
norms, data, concepts, feelings, and behavioural.
It is suggested that facilitators could think out
their strategy as to which forms of feedback would
be most appropriate in a given situation.

15 Self development activities for developing feedback strategies

These self development activities are designed
to explore the various feedback forms
described in Chapter 14. As with previous
self development activities some options are
described which are arranged in a logical
order. As before work pages are provided so
that you can develop your own ideas and
capture what has worked for you, as a result
of the suggested experimentation.

MENU OF ACTIVITIES

Activity 17, finding the 'gold bricks'. An
experiment in looking for significant events within
an interaction as the first step in generating
meaningful feedback.

Activity 18, picking up the 'gold bricks' an
experiment in using the observation of significant
events to generate feedback.

Activity 19, identifying various forms of feedback.
Practice as an observer.

<u>Activity 20,</u> generating various forms of feedback in a situation where you are facilitator.

ACTIVITY 17 FINDING THE 'GOLD BRICKS'

Process

1. Gain access to a skill development activity as an observer or obtain a video recording of such an activity.
2. Look for and note each 'gold brick'.
3. Note whether these were picked up or not, and if so, how.
4. Reflect on how you would have done it.

1. Gaining access

You will either need direct access to any interpersonal skill development activity in which you can observe what is going on, or obtain a video recording of a skill development session. It must of course contain the elements of interaction followed by feedback, but providing these are present, any sort of interpersonal skill development activity should be adequate.

2. Finding the 'gold bricks'

Watch the interaction very carefully and identify the significant events during the interaction which could form the basis of significant and meaningful feedback. These events might be things someone said, or reactions to what someone said or did. Body language can be very important in identifying significant events. An example could be during a discussion of an issue in a small group, when one member cuts across another member of the group, who gives signals of annoyance (frown, dismissive gesture, etc.). At the very least there are likely to be feelings data around at that moment in time. List these as you watch, for use in the next stage in this activity.

3. How are they picked up?

As you continue to watch the feedback part of the session look out for three things.

(a) How many of the significant events you noticed got picked up and how was this done?
(b) Were there any significant events which the

facilitator picked up and from which feedback
was developed which you did <u>not</u> notice?

(c)   Were there significant events which the
learners raised which you had <u>not</u> identified?
In practice I frequently find this to be the
case.

Reflection

Think about the process you have just followed and
the ways in which you could improve your ability to
identify significant events which could be a rich
source from which to generate feedback.

END OF ACTIVITY 17.

ACTIVITY 18 PICKING UP THE 'GOLD BRICKS'

Process

1. Set up a skill development session, video record if at all possible.
2. Pick up the 'gold bricks' and generate feedback.
3. Review the session.
4. Reflect on your successes/failures.

1. Set up the activity

This self development activity requires you to be in the role of facilitator. Any type of interpersonal skill development activity would do, structured exercises, role plays etc.. Clearly there would be an advantage in using one of the four approaches already described to give yourself more practice. As in other activities a video recording of the session is really essential to carry out the review.

2. Picking up the 'gold bricks'

As the session proceeds note the significant events and use these to both elicit and give feedback. Also try to get learners to identify significant events. It can be a good idea to see what the learners have noticed before you draw their attention to events that you have identified. For example, if you are using the 'stored' approach, and have remote control facilities on the video recorder you can give one of the group the responsibility for stopping the playback when they recall or notice something significant happening.

3. Review the session

Replay the video of yourself taking the session including both the activity and the feedback generation. Look for confirmation of the significant events which you recognised and which led to meaningful feedback being generated. Look also for significant events which the learners identified, which you did <u>not</u>, and look for the signals that you may have missed or misinterpreted. Link these observations with the feedback generated, and note any key phrases or other effective facilitating behaviour, which helped either the eliciting or giving of meaningful feedback. The format suggested on the work page should help to record useful notes and lead on to the last stage of this self development activity.

4. Reflect on success/failure

Reflect on your notes and identify what it was that successfully generated meaningful feedback and what was unsuccessful or less effective in this respect.

WORK PAGE

SIGNIFICANT EVENTS	SIGNALS THAT INDICATED THESE	HOW WAS FEEDBACK DEVELOPED	SUCCESSFUL/ UNSUCCESSFUL

ACTIVITY 19 IDENTIFYING VARIOUS FORMS OF FEEDBACK (AS AN OBSERVER)

Process

1. Gain access to an interpersonal skill development activity as an observer or obtain a video recording.
2. Identify the different forms of feedback being generated.
3. Identify the ways in which the feedback was generated.
4. Reflect on how you would handle such a session.

1. Gaining access

As with Activity 17 the intention of this activity is to practice observation and identification only. This is part of <u>your</u> awareness raising. The comments given in Activity 17 apply. It is unlikely that all the forms of feedback will be visible in any one session. This may be because of the type of interpersonal skill being developed, or the learners, or the preference or lack of experience of the facilitator. It would be very useful to repeat this activity with different facilitators and different groups, so that as far as possible a wide range of feedback forms can be identified.

2. Identifying the forms of feedback

Use the classification given in Chapter 14 viz.:

Reinforcement
Group norms
Data
Conceptual
Feelings
Behavioural

3. Identifying the ways of generating the feedback

As you identify each example of feedback generation (elicited or given) note how it has been facilitated, again capturing key phrases or other in facilitating behaviour used by the tutor. Tie these together using the format given on the next work page as the beginning of your personal collection of examples.

4. Reflection

Collect any data you can about learning that was a result of the session. Think about how well the choice of feedback form fitted the learner group and the learning goals of the session. How many forms were used and which ones were missing. From this, what other sessions should you be looking for or which forms of feedback do you now most want to experiment with.

FORM OF FEEDBACK	KEY PHRASES USED TO GENERATE FEEDBACK	DESCRIPTION OF LEARNING

ACTIVITY 20 GENERATING VARIOUS FORMS OF FEEDBACK

Process

1. Set up an interpersonal skill development activity which can be video recorded.
2. Generate appropriate and varied forms of feedback.
3. Review the session.
4. Reflect on your success/failures.

1. Set up the activity

As with Activity 18 you need to set up a skill development activity in which you are in the role of facilitator. Video record the session. The comments for Activity 18 are appropriate.

2. Generate the feedback

Try and vary the form of feedback you are using either by running different sessions using different forms, or by using more than one form in a session. This will enable you to test appropriateness.

3. Review the session

Replay the video of the session, and confirm the various forms of feedback you have been using and note key phrases you used to generate them. If feasible use the learner questionnaire from Activity 6. Using the work page format in Activity 19 add to your collection of successful facilitating activities.

4. Reflection

Think about what you have learned so far, and what other forms of feedback you would like to experiment with next. Review your work pages and notes and add to these if appropriate.

END OF ACTIVITY 20.

16 Questions of structure, openness and trainer role

Deals with issues of structure, openness, and
the choices available, and the role of the
tutor where choice may be contingent on a
number of factors.

INTRODUCTION

In the previous chapters emphasis has been placed
on designs which are based on the principles of
whole cycle learning. A number of specific
approaches and their variations have been
suggested, which to some readers may suggest rigid
structure, and facilitator dominance. However, the
approaches do not imply a particular level of
facilitator dominance nor a particular level of
closed educational design. The design and the
facilitator's behaviour can be dominant or exactly
the opposite. The design may be very open or
conversely very closed. A great deal of choice and
variation is possible within the approaches
suggested.

STRUCTURE

The question of structured, as opposed to unstructured designs, for interpersonal skill development activities is one of considerable debate. One issue is whether there is a clearly discernible structure present in a skill development activity, and whether this inhibits or facilitates learning. For example, in the Pfeiffer and Jones books of structured experiences, clear structures are set out and implemented by the facilitator (Pfeiffer and Jones, 1975). These structures include the process and methods for the learning activity as well as descriptions of materials and details of facilitator participation. At the other end of the spectrum T Groups are often cited as examples of unstructured small group activity, where learning may be orientated towards affective rather than skill development. In such activity the possibility that some structure may emerge or be suggested at some point does not detract from the general intention that a particular structure is not premeditated. The issue may therefore be not only if structure is present, but whether it is premeditated or not, and who puts it in. My personal stance on this issue is a purely contingent one. If certain structures are conducive to learning of a particular type, then I use them in a generally premeditated manner. If they begin to get in the way, then I encourage the group to find their own, but monitor the effect.

The approaches described in Chapter 8, 9 11, and 12 involve premeditated structure set up by the facilitator. The reasons why this is necessary are:

(a) To ensure that whole cycle learning takes places. This is not to deny that whole cycle learning is not possible without structure, but Kolb's work suggests that for most people, learning cycles will be unbalanced. Thus in a group of learners there may only be a minority who would naturally follow through a complete cycle of learning.

(b) Groups seem to need to learn how to learn for skill development. A good deal of emphasis

has been given to 'learning how to learn'
recently. Looked at from one perspective what
this means in reality is that people recognise
what part of their learning cycle they are
operating, and are thus able to manage this.
This should lead to the structure being
adopted by the group rather than imposed by
the facilitator. This implies of course that
the structure needs to be there in the first
place.

(c)   The learners need to establish themselves as a
learning group. The structure described in
this monograph encourages active participation
for all the group members. For example, a
group member may be observing an interaction,
then be called upon to give feedback, suggest
alternative behaviour, and then model this.
By using this structure the resource of all
the group members is utilised and the group
learns not only to recognise these resources,
but to value and use them.

The transition from a facilitator imposed
structure to the structure being adopted by the
learners is an important measure of learning within
the group. In practice using the approaches
described, this is likely to happen within 3 to 5
sessions of this form of skill development
activity. Some of the manifestations of this
happening are:

*   learners volunteering feedback (rather than
    being asked);
*   learners giving the appropriate form of
    feedback (e.g. genuine feelings rather than
    descriptions of what happened, 'that approach
    really nauseated me' instead of 'I thought you
    were a bit too polite');
*   learners missing out the step of describing
    alternative behaviour and moving straight into
    modelling without being asked by the
    facilitator ('I've got an idea, let me see if I
    can show you what I mean');
*   the original 'actor' asking to have another go
    rather than being persuaded by the facilitator;
*   where video playback is used, when the group
    takes control of the episodes or incidents they

want to comment on.

Such a development in a group has considerable
influence on the facilitator role as will be
discussed a little further on in this Chapter.
Thus to summerise, using the approaches described,
the structure needs to be established from the
outset, but if the group is working well, it should
be adopted rather than imposed after the group has
got used to it. The rate at which this may happen
will depend on the maturity of the group members as
learners.

OPENNESS

Open learning is much in evidence these days, the
Open University, the 'Open Tech' programme of the
Manpower Services Commission etc. (Tolley, 1983).
There tends to be some confusion about what
'openness' really means and in particular how open
learning relates to distance learning. Should the
Open University really be called the Distance
University? My own resolution of this problem is
to consider 'openness' and 'distance' as two
separate dimensions of learning (Binsted 1985).
This means in practice that a learning activity can
be either 'open' or 'distance' or neither or both.
It also implies that as these are dimensions,
activities may not be either wholly open or wholly
distance.

In considering skill development activities
openness implies choice by the learner. Choice
about learning goals, topics, process, and being
able to make up their own minds about what is usful
and applicable to themselves. The approaches
described in this monograph do not imply either
openness or non-openness. Examples have been given
of both. If openness is present then learners can
choose what situations and skills to work on, can
take charge of their own process, draw their own
conclusions, and finally decide what they are going
to do 'for real' back on the job.

If on the other hand a non-open situation is
required, where for instance a close check is
required on the learner's ability to demonstrate the

acquisition of particular specified skills, then
this can be achieved by the facilitator using
prepared models of 'correct' behaviour (film or
video) giving evaluative feedback and generally
enacting conditioning theories of learning. The
differences can be highlighted in tabular form, see
Table 16.1.

TABLE 16.1

OPENNESS	NON-OPENNESS
Learners:	Facilitator:
Choose problem situations	Defines situations
Identify skills to work on	Defines and specifies skills
Decide on what constitutes effective behaviour	Specifies effective behaviour
Receive non-evaluative feedback from group	Gives evaluative feedback
Experiment and explore	Organises practice drill and test
Manage their own process	Controls process
Enact experiential theories of learning	Enacts conditioning theories

FACILITATOR ROLE

As can be judged from the sections on structure and
openness although structure is present, the
facilitator has considerable choice about what role
to take, and in particular how to carry out the
role. At one extreme s(he) may be highly

controlling and at the other, very 'laid back' allowing complete freedom to the learner(s) to choose and decide on future behaviour. It is possible to identify facilitator roles which are primarily facilitating and those which are primarily controlling. The tutor may not have a free choice in the matter because for example of a need for uniform standardised behaviour. There appears to be a strong link between the facilitator adopting a controlling role and non-openness and imposed structure on the one hand, and a facilitating role and openness and adopted structure on the other. There are a number of consequences resulting from this choice.

The Controlling Role

In an extreme case this involves the facilitator in taking total responsibility for the learning activity. In some of our research it was found that responsibility could be defined in terms of topic, truth of content, and process (Binsted and Snell, 1981). Topic responsibility taken by the facilitator meant that what was learned was specified by him/her. Responsibility for truth of content, if taken by the facilitator, means that (s)he would be the arbiter of what was correct/incorrect, acceptable/unacceptable. Responsibility for process involves controlling the process throughout. The implication of the facilitator taking total responsibility is that the learners take none. Under these circumstances the facilitator must be able to specify the effective behaviour exactly, identify the relevant skills, and generally provide models of the correct way to act. As has been discussed in previous chapters this can be difficult to do for all but the simplest skills where uniformity of behaviour is feasible. For the more sophisticated skills used by managers and professionals, the facilitator may find the controlling role (in the extreme case) difficult to sustain.

The Facilitating Role

Again, trying to exemplify the role by taking the extreme case, the learner would take responsibility for choosing the topics to work on, and would

decide on appropriate of behaviour (= truth of
content) and would take joint responsibility with
the tutor for process. If the facilitator is
working with a sophisticated group, as an outsider
to the organisation, where there is a high
technological or knowledge content to interactions
(sales people in computers or pharmaceuticals,
doctor-patient, etc.), then the facilitator may
have little option, but to take a purely
facilitating role.

Appropriate Decisions

Taking a contingent view, the competent facilitator
would need to operate over a spectrum of roles,
depending on the area of skills to be developed,
the maturity of the learner(s), and his/her own
style. This would apply to the trainer running a
formal workshop or a manger involved in a coaching
session.

Concerning the choice of topic or situation to
work on, it would be entirely appropriate for the
facilitator to specify situations which were about
to arise due to organisational decisions, or policy
change (e.g. selling a new product or a new market,
people involved in new procedures or administering
new rules).

If on the other hand the learners have experience
of the interactions to be worked on, it could be
much more productive to get them to identify problem
areas (always remembering that they may have blind
spots). An example already given, of a group
generating an agenda in the group coaching situation
together with the use of instant interactive case
studies would exemplify this type of event.

Concerning the choice of what constitutes
effective behaviour, the key issue would appear to
be whether the facilitator is able to make valid
judgements. So for example a manager coaching a
subordinate new to the job would be able to do so,
whereas a facilitator on a workshop with a stranger
group working in a specialist area probably would
not. Concerning the choice of process, although
this occurs within a structure there is still room

for choice, and this is most likely to be a
function of learner maturity.

As a general rule of thumb, encouraging the
learner(s) to take as much responsibility as they
are able or willing to take, seems in practice to
be advantageous. Wellins and Guinn describe 'new
generation' behaviour modelling as being more
learner managed and suggest ways of doing this
while still using a conditioning based approach
(Wellins and Guinn, 1985). Although the approach
described in this monograph has a defined and
premeditated structure, this does not of itself
prescribe the extent to which the session can be
'open' nor does it prescribe facilitator's role.

SUMMARY

The approach already described suggests structure,
which will have to be imposed to start with but can
become adopted by learners. Sessions can be made
open or not, and this dimension is independent of
the method. Similarly the facilitator may adopt a
controlling or facilitating role although
circumstances may pre-empt this choice.

17 Application of the approach in organisations

How the approaches can be introduced into
organisations, or to individual facilitators.
Details of facilitator workshops and a
research project to monitor results.

INTRODUCTION

This Chapter will deal with the introduction of the
approaches described, to individuals and
organisational groups. It is based on a research
project carried out for a multi-national company,
and various other work for other multi-nationals
and some heterogeneous groups. In some cases
individuals were seeking to develop new ideas and
skills to apply to their own work situations, and
saw the approach as a useful additional tool.
Others were in fact attempting to institutionalise
the approach in their organisation. Most of the
Chapter is concerned with institutionalising the
approach with managers since this is the more
difficult thing to do. It was also the basis for
the formal research project.

TRAINERS AND TEACHERS

One group of people I have worked with are trainers from within organisations and some teachers (from Universities and Polytechnics). The trainers have been very much in the majority. For this group a workshop has been used to introduce the ideas and to develop their skill to use the approaches described in this monograph. Some have been run as open workshops for heterogeneous stranger groups, while others have been run for family groups of trainers, who all work within one organisation. This latter grouping is more effective for a number of reasons:

*   they all share a common culture, background and problems;
*   they thus have a unity of interest which focuses the learning into areas of mutual concern;
*   there is a team development spin-off;
*   the sharing of common experiences allows for dialogue at a deeper level around the issues raised;
*   the group can be encouraged to continue their own development and manage their own learning process.

All the people whether in heterogeneous or family groups were experienced trainers or teachers who had worked on interpersonal skill development. Thus they were enhancing and adding to existing skills rather than developing from a non-skill position. These workshops need to last 3 to 4 days. The design of the workshop was, of course, modelled on the approach since it was itself a skill development activity. The name of the game was to develop the trainer's skills to develop interpersonal skills in others. This presented some interesting design problems, e.g.:

(a) whether to aim for cognitive understanding of the approaches followed by practical work, which seemed to follow some logic. This was the design I first used, but quickly abandoned. The less I attempted to describe the processes and the various options the better it got. This got to the point of

189

abandoning any attempt to explain the process
and start straight in with a demonstration of
45 to 60 minutes, taking the facilitator role
myself with the workshop participants being
genuine learners. I now always generate the
issue to work on from the group (which is thus
owned and 'real') and either demonstrate the
'episodic' or the 'group coaching' approach,
and operate in the most non-directive role
that the group will tolerate. I then explore
the process and approach we have just
experienced, and explain the rationale of the
design and the learning process;

(b) how to establish a learning process that uses
the approaches being practiced and
experimented with. Having demonstrated the
approach and got some understanding of the
rationale behind it, a number of sessions are
scheduled for the group members to take a
session in the role of facilitator. It must
be emphasised that this is not a role play
situation. The workshop participants are
encouraged to work on real work problems and
situations. Thus in each small group one
person becomes facilitator and the rest of the
group become learners. To develop skills in
this facilitator, I need to focus the group's
attention on the facilitator skills and
behaviour. There are thus two levels of
process operating. Level 1 is the learning
process that the facilitator is facilitating,
which results in some level of skill
development in the 'learner' group. Level 2
is the learning process that I facilitate
which results in some level of skill
development in the whole group. A simple
example may clarify this.

A group of 6 trainers are attending a
workshop. One of the 6 takes the role of
facilitator and generates a 'real life'
problem that the group has energy to work on.
This turns out to be the problem of training
some managers to deal with giving some
negative feedback to a subordinate who is
rejecting and denying the data. The
facilitator sets up a session with one member

190

of the group taking the role of a manager and
another member of the group taking the role of
the subordinate. The other 3 members of the
group operate as observers initially, but get
involved in other roles as the session
progresses. The level 1 process is thus
facilitated by the facilitator who may choose
the 'episodic' approach. The outcome should
be that the group genuinely learns something
about how to deal with 'difficult'
subordinates. The level 2 process,
facilitated by me, will focus on the
facilitating behaviour used by the
facilitator. The outcome will be that the
group has learned something about running
skill development activities using the
episodic approach.

<u>It is of vital importance to separate the two
levels of process, otherwise confusion reigns</u>.

SEPARATING THE PROCESSES

There is really no choice at this point, the stored
approach is the only one feasible. The process I
set up (to practice what I preach) has 4 stages.

<u>Stage 1</u>, get the group working with one member
taking the role of facilitator. Videotape
facilitator behaviour and log important
interventions so that they can be subsequently
found. N.B. the focus is on facilitator behaviour,
exclusively. Let the facilitator complete the
session. Shown diagrammatically, the process at
this stage looks as in Figure 17.1.

Me   Facilitator   M   S

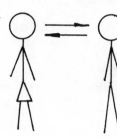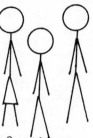

Taking   Set up   Interaction.   3 other
video   and   M taking role of   learners as
of   facili-   Manager, S as   observers
facili-   tate   subordinate   (at start)
tator   process
behaviour

Figure 17.1

Stage 2, ask each group member to write down what
they have learned about the topic they have just
worked on. In our example that could be triggered
by the question 'What have you learned about dealing
with subordinates who reject negative feedback'. I
generally ask the facilitator to also record what
learning (s)he <u>intended</u>.

Stage 3, generate feedback by asking the group to
share what they have learned. This is very
significant feedback about the effectiveness of the
session and sets a background for them moving into
the stored approach, which can be shown
diagrammatically as in Figure 17.2.

Me

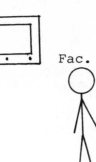

Fac.

Facilitating
video based
stored approach
focusing on F
interventions
only

Getting
feedback
etc.

Other learners in many
roles, interacting as
F, observers,
learners, etc.

Figure 17.2

<u>Stage 4</u>, ask the group to write down what they have
learned about running the episodic approach to
interpersonal skill development.

There can still be contamination between the two
processes, but this can generally be resolved by
alerting the group to what is going on. A space of
3 to 4 hours is required for one complete cycle of
learning, provided the part facilitated by the
learner facilitator (F) is restricted to 1 hour.
There is in general a strong demand for all the
learners on a workshop to have a turn at being F,
and this thus dictates the logistics of the whole
workshop, and defines the limit of group size and
number of staff facilitators required.

MANAGERS

All the work I have done with managers involved
developing their coaching skills. The differences
I have found are:

*   they often had low facilitation skills and were

not used to or familiar with developing
interpersonal skills in others;
* they all had considerable experience of dealing
with subordinates, in a managing rather than a
coaching role;
* they did not like theory or jargon;
* there was an intention by their company to
institutionalise an approach.

Developing these coaching skills was done through
workshops.

PRE WORKSHOP PREPARATION

In one company the senior manager functionally
responsible, the head of training and the training
staff attended a 3 day workshop to experience and
evaluate the approach. They became very positive
as a result and set up a subsequent workshop for
their area managers. One factor was that the
senior functional manager was very open minded and
willing to experiment. When it was his turn to
'have a go' at being facilitator, he performed in a
quite exemplary manner, the like of which I have
never since seen. This was an important factor in
convincing himself and the group that this was a
worth while approach. In another company, the
process started with a workshop for the trainers
from their European locations. Part of the
workshop involved a demonstration session of group
coaching. This led to a decision by the trainers
from the U.K. and some of the other locations to
run coaching skills workshops for their sales
managers. These were set up and resourced by one
or two of their trainers plus myself.

The U.K. workshops got off to a bad start, and it
was discovered that briefing had been very poor in
some cases. People had been sent sometimes at very
short notice, and all participants had overfull
work schedules. An even more important factor was
that none of them thought that coaching was part of
their job. 'Since when! When are we supposed to
do that etc.!' and worse still in a heavily results
orientated organisation 'Is this a new factor in
our staff appraisal system'. Senior managers, in
the shape of the U.K. Sales Manager and the

Regional Managers had to sort this out and improve the briefing and this solved the problem although people were still 'sent'.

The next thing to happen was that the managers attending demanded to know why their superiors were not attending the workshops and coaching them. That led to running a workshop for Regional Managers and the U.K. Sales Manager, and over a period all the managers were covered.

THE WORKSHOPS

These followed the emerging design already described. Having got over the insufficient briefing problem already described.

In the European locations, a series of workshops were run and difficulties were anticipated because all the participants had English as a second language. However, their standard was very high since English was the official company language, and the majority found no difficulty and expressed surprise that problems had not been more acute.

FOLLOW UP

In the case of the last mentioned company, this was done by the internal trainers. In the other company already referred to a comprehensive evaluation was undertaken by us. This involved collecting data from area managers and feeding this back in a follow up workshop. Later a sample of the people being coached were interviewed, the data was analysed and made anonymous and fed back to their area manager in a one day personal counselling session. This was done in 4 out of the 7 areas. All the data was then compounded, given further anonymity and fed back to the total group in another one day workshop.

In both organisations it was found that as skills improved learners did not know enough or have adequate theories about what constituted effective behaviour. Both took subsequent action to correct that.

FINDINGS AND CONCLUSIONS FROM THE FORMAL RESEARCH
(ONE ORGANISATION)

Some of the principle conclusions were:

*   size of group. Most managers found their
    normal group of 8 to 10 too large to handle at
    first. This was overcome by splitting the
    groups into two halves;
*   role playing. Everybody was familiar with role
    playing in the context of company training
    courses. Some groups recognised what was being
    done using the approaches, as different from
    role play, while others saw it as similar.

    Reasons why people saw it as similar to
    traditional role play were:

    (a) if the manager used words like role play,
         and did not emphasise that they were to
         either be themselves or reproduce behaviour
         of someone they knew;
    (b) if the manager set up situations for their
         group to work on, which the subordinates
         did not see as being their current
         problems (no ownership);
    (c) setting up the sessions within a formal
         conference setting.

    About 50% of the subordinates found some
    blocking off of learning when a strong role play
    message was received. It should be emphasised
    that the other 50% found the sessions
    satisfactory.

*   Non role playing. As changes were made and
    managers became more adept at using the method
    it became clear that these problems could be
    reduced by:

    (a) talking about trying out different ways of
         doing things and being yourself or someone
         else;
    (b) generating the problems and agendas from
         the learners;
    (c) setting up informal situations which
         learners described as 'sharing our
         experience, or sharing anecdotes'. It was

significant that when groups operated in
this way no one mentioned role play.

* Threat. Some found the situation as
threatening, talking about how things ought to
be done is one thing, but modelling it is very
different. Avoiding the former is, of course,
the whole purpose of the approach. This
element of threat became rather counter
productive in the formal situations especially
when 'Head Office' people were present and were
seen as having set it all up. Some felt their
ability to model was actually being assessed.
These problems disappeared when an area family
group met on its own, even though it was still
their immediate boss who was doing the
coaching.

* What to do with the highly experienced learner,
who does not need anymore training (or so he
thinks). Using the approaches described allows
the coach (in a group coaching situation) to
use superior skills and expose them by asking
the experienced person to model behaviour.
'You've done a lot of this sort of thing Fred,
show us how you do it'. This allows the
experienced person to feel useful and
motivated, and raises their self esteem. It is
possible that a person whose self esteem is
already too high may demonstrate a level of
skill rather below what was predicted, which
can be a highly significant though perhaps
uncomfortable learning experience.

* How to use the approaches. Two main uses
emerged:

    (a) as ways of exploring problems experienced
         in the field, sometimes when the manager
         was present. This got the highest rating
         for effectiveness;
    (b) as a way of working through problems that
         were about to occur because of some new
         situation or change. Some groups made
         realistic action plans in this way.

* The experiential learning model. As a result
of this research the model was constructed

which suggests two dimensions to learning
situations involving learning from learner
interactions, and sheds light on the issues
surrounding role. The model is shown in Figure
17.3

The two dimensions are:

1.   learner perception of the familiarity of
      the situation. This may be entirely
      different from the tutor's perception, and
      may vary from familiar (e.g. a common work
      problem) to unfamiliar which may be being
      oneself to acting out a script;

2.   motivation for learner behaviour.

The four corners of the model represent four
different learning situations:

<u>Playing/acting</u> represents the better form of
role play.
<u>Fantasy/farce</u> represents what a badly designed
role play degenerates into.
<u>Experimenting</u> represents a useful exploration
of new and unfamiliar situations.
<u>Natural</u> is the way of learning by working
through real problems.

The dimension of reality is shown diagonally,
real being at the 'natural' corner, unreal
being at the fantasy/farce corner.

Effective transferable learning will be most
likely in the natural corner. Little or no
learning is likely in the fantasy/farce corner,
and should be avoided. When setting up a
situation it is generally quite easy to use the
model to predict the learning situation which
is likely to develop.

   In conclusion it can be seen that the experience
and research findings of using the approaches has
been incorporated in the description and comment in
earlier Chapters. Overall there is evidence that
people quite rapidly get used to the approach, but
as with all types of training, the way it is
introduced and the conditions under which it is used

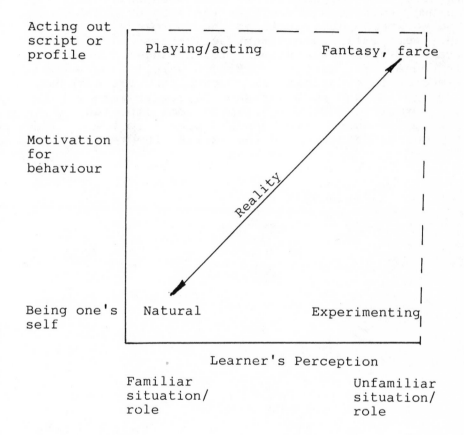

Figure 17.3 A Model of Experiential Learning

are of vital importance. Hence the emphasis of not
creating barriers to learning by long and
threatening explanations of process, imposed
topics, etc.

SUMMARY

The ways in which the approaches have been
introduced to organisations have been initially
through workshops for either trainers or managers.
The workshops have utilised the approaches since
they were skill development activities. The
trainer workshops were both for stranger groups and
in house. The manager workshops were in house and
aimed at institutionalising coaching. Pre workshop
preparation and post workshop follow up were vital.
The formal research highlighted some important
principles which have been fed back into the
approaches described in the earlier Chapters.

18 Future developments

Introducing the approaches into your sphere of
work, and the possibilities of self
development groups and distance learning
packages.

VARIATIONS ON THE THEME

It is to be hoped that you have not formed the view
that the approaches described are rigid procedures
that have to be adhered to, regardless of the
context in which they will be used or your own
preferences. Rather, I would hope that you have
understood the principles underlying the approaches
and have some ideas about what makes them work.
There will be a number of factors which will
influence your plans about what you want to do
next. For example:

(a)   which form of approach will be appropriate for
        your culture, or the culture of your client?
        Do you have to be directive or can you be
        experimental and exploratory? Do not be
        worried if you cannot understand all the

technical content of the learner's
interactions.

(b) Are the learners mature and experienced enough
     to produce 'instant case studies'? A trial
     run should soon establish that.

(c) How will you introduce the new approaches, by
     integrating some of the ideas with more
     traditional approaches or by a clear change to
     the approaches described? If the latter,
     doing it without explanation 'naturally' seems
     to work best.

(d) How are you going to enhance your skills as a
     facilitator? If you have done all the self
     development exercises you should be well on
     the way.

SELF DEVELOPMENT GROUPS

Once a learner group has got used to the process of
learning embodied in the approaches, you will
generally find that they begin to take on some of
the facilitating behaviour required to maintain the
process. For example, in modelling alternative
behaviour, the group may start from a situation
where the facilitator has to actively persuade a
learner to 'show the group what he means' following
a verbal suggestion of an alternative behaviour.
The process is quickly recognised by the learners
and may then become a bit of a game. Learners may
produce a token show of reluctance 'I should have
kept my mouth shut'. This often develops into
learners volunteering to model behaviour, 'I'd like
to try something'. If the facilitator only elicits
feedback it is possible to reduce the role until
the point where the group can handle its own
process. At this point the facilitator can at
least in theory withdraw and the learners can
become a self development group. There is then the
possibility of flipping into and out of the process
very quickly and informally. Two or more people
can constitute such a group. Such a group can
rapidly try out ideas and constructively develop
them, for example as preparation for a
presentation, negotiation, or customer visit.

Motivation and support will be vital issues.

DISTANCE LEARNING

There is growing interest in distance learning as a means of developing people. In the interpersonal skill area some work has been done, but developments are at an early stage. The development of interactive video systems offers significant potential for interpersonal skill development. The question is whether or not the learning process and principles described in this monograph can be accommodated in an interactive video system. On the face of it there seems to be no reason why not. Thinking of the three elements of the learning process:

1. Modelling behaviours presents no problem. Video is the perfect medium for doing this. All that would be required would be short sequences of one episode length with a collection of alternative behaviours, which could be selected by the learner in various ways.

2. Reflection also produces no problem. All that would be necessary would be to put in appropriate pages of computed generated text such as 'Note any ideas that you think could use from the video sequences you have just seen'.

3. Discovery on first sight appears to be the most problematical because what is needed is for the learner to be involved in a live interaction on which she can get feedback. A simple solution to the first problem suggests itself. First there would need to be two or more learners interacting with the programme. This should not present any great problem in a work based learning situation. Research into the effectiveness of computer based learning suggests that there is often an advantage in two or more learners engaging together in a programme. It takes longer but the learning quality shows improvement.

Second, a video camera would be required to feed into the video cassette recorder used in the interactive video system. At this point in time this excludes video disc systems. At an appropriate point the computer generated text will prompt the learners to set up an interaction between themselves which will be recorded on what is in effect a blank bit of tape (in fact it will be erasing and over recording the last learner's contribution). This will take care of the 'action' element of the discovery loop. Generating the feedback again at first sight seems problematical. Three sources are available:

(a)   the learners themselves. All that should be required is for a page of computed generated text to prompt the feedback process using similar words to those a facilitator would use;
(b)   the recorded interaction the learners have made, which can be reviewed at any point in the programme;
(c)   pre-recorded sequences which can be viewed, compared and analysed.

Modelling alternative behaviour can be achieved as in the approaches already described by getting the learner group to do it or using pre-recorded sequences. May I hasten to add that these ideas have not been proved in practice but research on them is currently being done at Lancaster.

USES OF DISTANCE LEARNING

There appear to be two obvious directions for developing distance learning:

1.   For learners who want to develop interpersonal skills in any appropriate area.

2.   For facilitators who wish to develop facilitating skills for face to face interpersonal skill development.

   If you have done the text based self development

activities based in this monograph you may be able
to form an opinion about how useful an interactive
video package would be.

From a theoretical point of view there does
not appear to be any reason why the principles
already expounded in this monograph could not form
the basis for an interactive video design. In
practice I anticipate a number of awkward but not
insoluable problems, mainly stemming from the fact
that to my knowledge no one has thought of trying
to solve them.

SUMMARY

This last Chapter raises some questions about how
to go about introducing the approaches into your
work situation, and suggests further developments
where the principles can be used for self
development groups and in distance learning
packages.

Bibliography

Argyris, C. and Schon, D.A., <u>Theory into Practice:</u>
  <u>Increasing Professional Effectiveness</u>,
  Jossey-Bass, 1976.
Baker, D. and Phillips, K., 'Transactional
  Analysis' in Cooper, C.L. (ed.), <u>Improving</u>
  <u>Interpersonal Relations</u>, Addison Wesley, 1977.
Barnard, R., 'Developing Management-Trainer
  Skills-Feedback', <u>BACIE Journal,</u> January 1980.
Berne, E., <u>Games People Play</u>, Penguin, 1964.
Binsted, D., 'The Management Teacher: Some
  Investigations into Management Teachers and the
  Environments in Which They Work', <u>Research Report</u>
  <u>No. 8</u>, CSML, University of Lancaster, 1977.
Binsted, D., 'Design for Learning in Management
  Training and Development: A View', <u>Journal of</u>
  <u>European Industrial Training</u>, vol. 4, no. 8,
  1980.
Binsted, D., 'Open and Distance Learning and the
  New Technologies' in <u>Handbook of Management</u>
  <u>Development,</u> Gower, 1985.
Binsted, D. and Snell, R., 'The Tutor-Learner
  Interaction in Management Development, Part 1.
  The Effect of Relationships and Tutor
  Facilitating Strategy on Feelings, Learning and

Interest', <u>Personnel Review,</u> vol. 10, no. 3,
1981.
Binsted, D. and Snell, R., 'The Tutor-Learner
Interaction in Management Development Part 5.
Facilitating Learning from the De-Briefing of
Exercises', <u>Personnel Review</u>, vol. 11, no. 4,
1982.
Blake, R.R. and Mouton, J.S., <u>The Managerial Grid</u>,
Gulf, 1964.
Bloom, B.S. (ed), 'Taxonomy of Educational
Objectives', Book 1, <u>Cognitive Domain</u>, Longman,
1972.
Bloom, B.S., Krathwohl, D.R., and Masia, B.B.,
'Taxonomy of Educational Objectives', Book 2,
<u>Affective Domain</u>, Longman, 1971.
Burgoyne, J.G., 'Management Learning Development',
<u>BACIE Journal</u>, vol. 31, no. 9, 1977.
Burgoyne, J.G. and Stuart, R., 'Implicit Learning
Theories as Determinants of the Effect of
Management Development Programmes', <u>Personnel
Review</u>, vol. 6, no. 2, 1977.
Cantor, N., <u>Dynamics of Learning</u>, 3rd edition,
Buffalo, Stewart, 1956.
Cover, W.H., 'Curbstone Coaching', <u>Training and
Development Journal</u>, November, 1980.
Dyer, D.A. and Giles, W.J., 'Interaction Analysis',
in Cooper, C.L. (ed.), <u>Improving Interpersonal
Relations</u>, Gower, 1981.
Gagne, R.M., <u>The Conditions of Learning</u>, second
edition, Holt, Rinehart and Winston, 1970.
Harris, T.A., <u>I'm O.K. You're O.K.</u>, Pan, 1969.
Israel, R., 'A New Approach to Sales Training:
Behaviour Modelling', <u>Personnel News and Views</u>,
vol. 7, no. 1, 1977, National Retail Merchants
Association, New York.
Jones, L., 'Positive Reinforcement', <u>Education and
Training</u>, June 1980.
Kagan, N., <u>Interpersonal Process Recall, Basic
Method and Recent Research</u>, CSML Conference Paper
1982.
Klein, R. and Smith, F., 'Supervisory Feedback in
Training', <u>Training and Development Journal</u>,
September 1981.
Kolb, D.A. and Fry, R., 'Towards an Applied Theory
of Experiential Learning', in Cooper, C.L. (ed),
<u>Theories of Group Processes</u>, John Wiley, 1976.
Megginson, D. and Boydell, T., 'A Manager's Guide
to Coaching', <u>BACIE Journal,</u> February 1981.

Morrison, J.H. and O'Hearne, J.J., Practical
  Transactional Analysis in Management, Addison
  Wesley, 1977.
Mumford, A. and Honey, P., The Manual of Learning
  Styles, Peter Honey, 1982.
N.T.L., Reading Book, Laboratories in Human
  Relations Training, 1969.
Pfeiffer, J.W., and Jones, J.E., A Handbook of
  Structured Experiences for Human Relations
  Training, vol. I-V, University Associates, 1975.
  (These volumes have been extended annually since
  then.)
Phillips, K. and Fraser, B., The Management of
  Interpersonal Skills Training, Gower, 1982.
Rackham, N. and Morgan, T., Behaviour Analysis in
  Training, McGraw-Hill, 1977.
Shaw, M.E., 'Sales Training in Transition',
  Training and Development Journal, February, 1981.
Singer, E.J., Effective Management Coaching,
  I.P.M., 1981.
Stuart, R., 'Towards Re-Establishing Naturalism in
  Management Training and Development', Journal of
  Industrial and Commercial Training, July/August,
  1984.
Thayer, L. and Beeler, K.D. (ed), Affective
  Education: Strategies for Experiential Learning,
  University Associates, 1976.
Tolley, G., 'The Open Tech, Why, What and How',
  Paper No. 1, Open Tech Programme, Manpower
  Services Commission, 1983.
Tosti, D.T., 'Behaviour Modelling: A Process',
  Training and Development Journal, August, 1980.
Wellins, R.S. and Guinn, K.A., Behaviour Modelling:
  A New Generation, Development Dimensions
  International, 1985.